THE
SPIRIT
OF
TRUTH

Arthur Katz
AND
Paul Volk

THE SPIRIT OF TRUTH

by Art Katz and Paul Volk

Copyright © 2008—Art Katz Ministries

Previously published under ISBN 1-878327-25-9

These and other materials of a comparable kind can be found at:

www.artkatzministries.org

ISBN 10 digit: 0-9749631-1-9
ISBN 13 digit: 978-0-9749631-1-2

Published by Burning Bush Press

Fifth American Printing, 2011

CONTENTS

From Fullness to Power
Test of Truth: Among Those Who Know Us
Bluffing vs. Substance
Judgment: To the Church First
Our Deepest Longing and Goal

Coming to a Full Stop
Pragmatism vs. Obedience
God's Plumb Line of Truth is Absolute
Heavenly Truth vs. Worldly Wisdom
Truth: A Moment by Moment Vigilance

Paul: An Israelite Indeed
Speaking Truth in the Power of the Spirit
Confidence in Truth vs. Human Ability
The End Dictates the Means
You Can Tell a Book by its Cover
The Subtleties of Deceit
The Spirit of Truth Allows No Compromise
Gentleness and Boldness: One Source
Only a Crucified Life …
Walking in Truth: The Choice of the Cross

Redefining the Part as the Whole
Abundant Grace and Wholeheartedness
Embracing the Whole Truth
The Fear of the God of Truth
Every Lie has Root in the Father of Lies
The Character of the King
Humility: Our Need—God's Provision
Who is Sufficient?...
What Goes Up Must First Go Down
Jesus' Triumphal Entry
Desiring His Humility More Than His Power
The New Jerusalem

Foreword

...the house of God, which is the church of the living God, *the pillar and the ground of the truth.* (*I Timothy 3:15*).

I suspect that in your experience, as in mine, the references to this foundational description of the Church have been rare. The omission may be significant, for the unhappy truth is, that of all the institutions of the earth, the Church is the most stilted and inauthentic, the most predictable and contrived.

How is it that a phenomenon whose origin is heavenly and was purchased at such cost should become, by our generation, so melancholy a culture? Is it not that we have failed to jealously prize and safeguard truth itself, instead of exercising the daily, moment-by-moment diligence that truth by its very nature requires? Have we not recognized that the issue of truth is so much more than mere outward compliance to form, that only the intensity of a lover of truth would suffice?

Appropriately enough, the essay that you are about to read had its origin at a church where I was brought one Sunday morning, free from any commitment of my own, to enjoy the luxury of hearing another preacher. I went tripping as a doe, full of delight and anticipation, buoyed by the lavish praise for the minister as a preacher of the Word, by the brother who escorted me.

I was seated in the balcony of the crowded church, attentive and waiting, but not a little disturbed by the contrasting groups around me. On the one hand, the assembly included clusters of giddy teenagers round about. On the other hand, I was struck by the air of religious stiffness and joylessness in

5

the adults. I endeavored to throttle my jaundiced subjectivity, not wanting in any way to allow it to impinge upon the preached word now beginning to come forth. As the message unfolded, I could readily understand the enthusiasm for the preacher that my companion held. The words were clear, pointed, and correct. What, then, was this strange uneasiness rising in my soul that intensified with every word, till finally my innards were knotted in an inexplicable anguish?

At last I realized my dilemma: my mind was approving the outward biblical and doctrinal correctness of the word preached, but my soul was recoiling at the spirit of the speaking that contradicted its every syllable! We were with the one enjoined to radical commitment and sacrifice, while the other was saying, "No need to panic; this need not be taken seriously—remember, this is only a sermon. I'll provide a biblical message weekly, and you provide for my personal security and well being. I won't push you, and you won't push me, and we'll get along famously."

In that moment, the realization was birthed in me (should I have not long before seen it?): *the truth is the whole truth and nothing but the truth, or it is not the truth.* The spirit of the one speaking—the constitution and grit of the person—must be in complete agreement with the words of the one speaking, or it is a lie. The devastating words of the widow of Zarephath to the prophet Elijah pierce me still:

"Now by this I know that thou art a man of God, and that the word of the Lord in thy mouth is truth." (I Ki 17:24 KJV).

So commenced the reflections, given as a series of messages, which you are about to read. My colleague in this endeavor is Paul Volk, like myself, a believer whom you would

6

likely have little occasion to know. Our souls have become intertwined in the years together in community here in northern Minnesota, where we have wrestled through the issues of the faith. We are Jews of an intellectual and academic bent, seeking to disengage the faith from its cultural and traditional trappings, so as to behold it and proclaim it in all purity. There are few men who better know my heart, and who are able to interpret and express it with an uncommon incisiveness and clarity. As his wife Adrienne has often expressed, "You can't tell where the one ends and the other begins."

Well, I *can* tell, for I am often left admiring, if not envying, the turn of a thought that Paul brings that converts an insight into an aphorism, so pithy and penetrating that the entire book is thereby justified. I am left with the strange feeling in reading this manuscript of something that is mine, yet not mine—intimately familiar, yet new. It is the synthesis of two minds and hearts and spirits that makes it qualitatively other and infinitely better; it is even a foretaste, if you will, of the glories of true corporateness that await the flowing together of the Body of Christ in this last hour. You be the judge. As I have frequently said, theology is too precious and expansive for the labors of one, but it needs a plurality of effort and insight to bring forth its beveled brilliance. May this book be an intimation of that, however modest.

Finally, may our effort kindle anew the love of truth that, in this dark and turbulent age of deception, alone saves one from perishing. The cynical spirit of Pontius Pilate that implies that truth cannot be known, or the spirit in our relativistic age that says truth does not even exist, increasingly pervades. It is a fashionable posture and presumption, which is itself a lie, that will contend against the truth even unto death. The love for the truth, which is its only antidote, will be costly in this hour. May the Lord, who Himself is Truth, breathe on these pages to inspire the courage to desire and seek the truth, to witness and obey it, to suffer for it as inevitably one must, so that, in the end, there might be a Church in this devious world that is the ground and pillar of Truth. May we be kept from that longing for the manifestations of the power of God that is unaware, as Jesse Penn-Lewis reminds us, that the Spirit of God, before He can be known or experienced as either power or love, is first and primarily, the Spirit of Truth.

Aruthur Katz
Laporte, Minnesota

Introduction

"What is Truth?" Pontius Pilate never asked a more important question. And, though the man of whom he asked it did not utter a single word in reply, no man ever received a more complete and articulate answer. Why was Jesus silent? And, when asked that same question by men today, why are we so compelled to speak? One would think we had at our disposal far more truths and right doctrines than Jesus had. We could have given Pilate a very impressive statementæall quite scriptural and correct. Why didn't Jesus do the same? At other times and in other encounters He was strikingly articulate. He could reason and contend with the best religious minds in Israel.

Yet before Pilate, Jesus, the master of encounter, the supreme scriptural debater, stood mute. His silence was not born of a lack of truths. He possessed truths in abundance. He was silent not because He lacked truths but because He was full of truth, because He was truth - and in that moment to utter a single truth would have been to obscure the living truth that He was. If Pilate could not see truth before him, in a light and clarity heightened by the silence in which it stood, then nothing he might have heard could have saved him. And that causes us to wonder if perhaps the reason we so often cannot abide in silence is that we fear that it would only make more apparent the absence rather than the presence of truth in ourselves.

Jesus may not have spoken to Pilate, but He did speak to us. He even answered for us the question that Pilate asked, but His answer was as perplexing and as contrary to our expectations as was His silence to Pilate. "I am the Truth...," He said, implying that *truth is more than a sum of right answers. It is not something to have at all but something, first and above all else, to be.* Truth is a spirit, a life; and this spirit, this life is the way, the only way to the Father. **"I am...the truth, and... no one comes to the Father but by me." (John. 14:6 RSV)**

Suddenly it dawns upon us that it is not by *having* truths but by *becoming* true that we are saved. God's desire is not merely to inform us but to transfigure us, not to fill us with truths but to make us true. The Holy Spirit, the Comforter, the Spirit of Christ, the Spirit of adoption which sheds God's love abroad in our hearts, is the Spirit of Truth.

Jesus leaves us on new, unfamiliar ground. We know what it means for a statement or a doctrine to be true, but what does it mean when a man declares, "I am the truth"? We know what it means to have truth but stagger at the idea of being true. We are far more at home with the religion that is occupied with having and doing. We know how to go about acquiring more and more truths. But the religion of God is animated foremost by a desire to be, not merely to do or acquire. *We seek to possess truth; God seeks to make us true. The difference is vast and the kinds of men produced by each pursuit are vastly different and will have a different effect.*

To believe that having is being, that becoming true is simply a function of acquiring a sufficient amount of truth, is a deception. What such deception produces, if allowed to go unbroken, is the tragic and ironic spectacle of men impeccable (so they think) in their doctrines, yet living lives that are essentially performance and imitation, which is to say, false. If a widow could say to Elijah, **"the Word of the Lord in your mouth is truth," (I Kings 17:24 NAS),** then it must follow that the Word of God in someone else's mouth can be false. The mouth, the voice, is not separate

10

from the word that comes out from it. Voice and word are an unbroken continuum. Jesus speaks God's word because He is God's word. He speaks truth because He is true. Truths are important but they are as dead, and as deadly, as the law written on stone, without the Spirit of Truth in us to animate them. If the Law alone, however correctly quoted and followed, could not make us righteous, how could truths alone, however orthodoxy professed, ever make us true? As Christ is the goal and fulfillment of God's law, so is He the goal and fulfillment of God's truths. The same God who could make a Pharisee like Paul into a living epistle of His grace by the Spirit of grace can also make His Church a living demonstration of truth by the Spirit of Truth.

This little book is intended to be something different from an exposition of biblical truths. Hopefully it will prove to be more then just another book *about* truth. It had its origin in a series of messages spoken over several days to a gathering of believers, messages that were meant to reveal and hopefully even demonstrate the very Spirit of Truth, who is the essence of all truths. It is often difficult enough to capture in writing truths once spoken. It is even more difficult to convey the spirit in which they were spoken. This book is meant to be true, in word and in spirit. It is intended to restore the unity between the word and the life of truth without which truth is cold and dead. If it only informs its readers it will have failed. If God can use it to some degree to transform them it will have succeeded.

However, a final word of caution may be necessary. The pages that follow consistently proclaim truth as a spirit, which is to say, something more than words. *Truth is indeed more than what we say; it ought to be what we are. But while truth is more than words, it is not less than words.* We live in an

11

age that increasingly despises and denigrates prepositional truth. Even within the Church it is becoming a source of embarrassment to contend for the doctrines of the faith, as if all contending was of necessity contentious, and who wants to be labeled divisive in our increasingly ecumenical age? Some seem to think that by putting the word "mere" before "doctrine" that the subject has been sufficiently dealt with. But there are no "mere" doctrines. The truths of the faith are and will continue to be worth living and dying for.

It would be a mistake to take the emphasis of this book about truth as a spirit as if it were in opposition to truth as word. *The Spirit of Truth needs to be proclaimed not because the word of truth is unimportant but precisely because it is so very important.* Truths woodenly proclaimed without a life that is true are a disservice to truth. But likewise the elevation of being "authentic" or "real" or "true" in a way that diminishes the place and value of the truths once given to the Church does an equal disservice to truth. This book is a cry for the whole truth. It would be tragic and a real irony if the Spirit of Truth ever became yet one further and final banner behind which a partial and therefore false version of truth was championed.

Paul Volk
St. Paul, Minnesota

12

CHAPTER 1

Walking in the Truth

**Beloved, I pray that in all respects you may prosper
and be in good health, just as your soul prospers.
For I was very glad when brethren came and bore
witness to your truth, that is, how you are walking
in truth. I have no greater joy than this, to hear of
my children walking in the truth.
(III Jn: 2-4 NAS).**

No Greater Joy

Of all the things that could possibly describe our relationship to truth, why did John choose walking? And what is it about walking in truth that causes John his greatest joy? There are grander expressions that could have been used, suggestive of something more lofty and spiritual. Walking is an activity so commonplace, so ordinary that we give it little, if any, thought. It is as unconscious as breathingæand that is just what makes it so important, so revealing. Walking is precisely the right word because it suggests nothing lofty or exalted. It brings truth down into the everyday, into every aspect of a person's life, which is where it belongs.

Walking is part of almost everything we do, whether we are walking to the refrigerator, or to the pulpit. There is hardly a word more inclusive, or, therefore, more appropriate to describe the conduct of our lives than "walking." It is no wonder, then, that John chose it to describe our relationship to truth; and it is no wonder that John, and we can safely add

God Himself, rejoices to see His children walking in truth. "I have no greater joy." Does it not follow, then, that His grief is to hear of His children, so knowledgeable in "truths," walking in pretense, deceit and lies?

Walking in truth is not something that just happens. Though it expresses itself so naturally and thoughtlessly, it is not attained without thought or by accident. Walking in truth happens just like walking itself, one step at a time. Choice by choice, moment by moment, one's abiding in truth or untruth is being determined. To affect a pose or not, to self-interestedly calculate the effect of a word or gesture or not, to say the "appropriate" but insincere thing or not, such choices present themselves over and over in the course of a day, and their cumulative effect is to render one habitually true or untrue. It would be a grave mistake to think that quoting scriptures correctly or subscribing to the right doctrines wholly constitutes walking in truth. A man may be saying all the right words, yet be contradicting his words by the insincere manner in which he says them. You hear him, and while your intellect is saying "true," your spirit is saying "false." It is possible to know the truth yet not walk in it, and the truth is really in us, and we in it, only to the degree that we actually walk in it.

Express Truth in All Things

The Amplified Bible renders a statement of Paul's from Ephesians like this: **"Let our lives lovingly express truth in all things, speaking truly, dealing truly, living truly" (Eph 4:15 Amplified).** Few statements capture the meaning of walking in truth so well. "All things" is all-inclusive. It is not possible to confine truth to our speaking and still fulfill what Paul is saying here. Our tendency is not to see our lives as a seamless whole, but rather as a patchwork of discreet fragments. We tend to compartmentalize everything. We live as if our health, both mental and physical, our faith, our doctrines, our relationships, all existed in distinct spheres, each with its own rules and regulations, quite isolated from and unrelated to each other. Thus, we dangerously misconceive our own nature as fragmentary and suffer because we do. It is no surprise, then, that we misconstrue the nature of truth itself and imagine it to pertain only to our doctrines and our thinking. It hardly occurs to us that truth is meant to pervade and express itself through every aspect of our lives, in all things, nor does it occur that each of our lives is a single whole through which truth should be expressed. The fact is, that it is truth, the Spirit of Truth, which unites and holds us together. By confining truth to a small verbal, doctrinal part of our lives, we condemn ourselves to being fragmented and full of internal opposition and contradictions, which is to say, we condemn ourselves to being untrue.

Walking is an activity, not of just feet, but of the whole body. If the whole body does not walk, then no part of it will either. **"Express truth in all things."** If we are not expressing it in all things, then are we really expressing it at all? We may be able to make true statements, but such verbal formulations are merely an effect of truth. They do not of themselves constitute its substance, its demonstration. Truth, because it is foremost a quality of life, a living spirit, requires a life through which to express itself. Truth must be lived, or it will cease to be truth. That is why it is our walking in truth, and nothing short of that, that causes John, as well as God Himself, to rejoice. **"I have no greater joy than to hear of my children walking in truth."**

A house divided against itself cannot stand, and a man divided within himself cannot stand either. Jesus came upon a man sitting beside the pool at Siloam, who had been crippled for 38 years, and asked him if he wanted to be made whole. What would our response be if He suddenly asked us the same question?

There are many of us who have been crippled for as long or longer, sitting in our "correct" understanding, but unable to walk in truth. In order to be able to walk in the Spirit of Truth, one must be made whole. Do we want to be made whole? When God comes and asks that question, He is asking about something far more than our health or our bank account; He is asking about our whole life. Do we want truth to drop like a plumb line into every area of our lives, revealing as well as righting every inconsistency? Do we want every false and deceptive thing removed so that we might speak truly, deal truly, and live truly? We all want to walk, but do we want to walk in the way and in the life? Jesus said, **"I am the way, and the truth, and the life; no one comes to the Father, but by Me."** **(Jn 14:6 NAS).** To be made whole, to be able to walk in this way, we need to cry out, not, "God, give me more truth," but, "God, make me true! Teach my heart to fear your name!"

A man walking in truth is not hard to recognize. He is consistently whole in marriage, ministry, work and worship. His wardrobe, medicine cabinet, and face do not contradict one another. That very wholeness and reality is truth itself, making itself known through someone's life—and it shows. Whenever the inner and outer lives have been brought into unity, it always shows. This is truth. This is salvation: a life set free from the burden and strain of trying to keep a disconnected life together, of being a different person at work, at church, at home, and alone. But do we want this much truth? Do we want this much salvation? Do we want this much of

God? To say, "I love truth," yet to want to be less than wholly true is itself a contradiction, just as it is a contradiction to say, "I love God," and yet not love Him with one's whole heart and mind and strength. Our love for God is really no greater than our love for truth. We have no more of one than of the other. Truth, like God, will not force itself upon us. It will penetrate only so far as we let it, and we will let it live in us only as much as we desire it, and desire to walk in it.

Silver-Plated Christians

Years ago, when silver dollars were really made of silver, there was a simple way to determine if they were genuine or not. All you had to do was throw them down and listen to the sound they made when they hit the ground. If a coin was an imitation, if it was merely silver-plated, though it might have given every appearance of being genuine, it made a dull thud when it hit the ground. By contrast the real silver dollar rang true because it was silver, not just on the outside, but all the way through. The imitation may have had real silver on the surface, but it was still worthless. It had to be of the same substance at its core as on its surface, or it was not a silver dollar at all.

Sadly, there are many "silver-plated Christians" in the Church today. There is a layer of real truth on the surface of our lives. We sound very scriptural. However, our actual condition, the true state of our inner man, is revealed, not by how biblically correct we are, but by the sound we make when we hit the ground. What happens when we are thrown down, that is, when we are thrust into an unexpected situation, adversity, or temptation? How do we respond when there is no time to compose a religious phrase or face? Does our life ring true at home, or at work, or when we are alone and no one sees or hears? What are our inward thoughts when we are free to think what we will? Are we silver through and through or only on the surface? In the Psalms, David expressed his own realization about truth as God reckons it. **"You desire truth in the innermost parts" (Ps 51:6),** David said to God. He understood at that moment what John expressed long after: God's greatest joy is reserved for his children who walk in the truth.

David's Deception

David wrote the fifty-first psalm as a result of a profound and painful revelation of his own innermost parts. The story is a familiar one. David had arranged to have Bathsheba's husband, Uriah, killed in battle rather than to have his adultery brought to the light. After a considerable time, Nathan the prophet went to David to confront him. He did so indirectly by first telling him a story. He related how a wealthy man, needing a lamb to slaughter to feed a guest, takes the one precious lamb of a poor neighbor. David's sense of justice was aroused, and in anger he pronounced stern judgment against the rich man. **"As the Lord lives, the man who has done this deserves to die; and he shall restore the lamb fourfold, because he did this thing and because he had no pity." (II Sam 12:5-6 RSV).** It was at this point, and not a moment before, that Nathan turned to David and said, **"Thou art the man!" (II Sam 12:7).**

A considerable time elapsed between David's sin and the day Nathan confronted him. Why didn't God send Nathan to David immediately? Why did He allow David to go on in his sin? The answer lies in David's own heart and in what he needed to see in himself. He presumably continued in the day-to-day activity as Israel's king, not to mention in his daily relationship with Bathsheba. How was that possible for him?

David had been terribly unjust, yet his sin did not prevent him from discerning and responding with great indignation towards the injustice of the rich man in Nathan's story. David was a man passionately committed to justice, while at the same time he himself was being unjust. The fact is, we are often as quick and fervent in discerning error in others as David was in his anger towards the man in Nathan's story. We can be fervent "men of truth" outwardly, while inwardly living a lie about ourselves and not know it. When Nathan said, "Thou art the man," David saw the breach between the inner and outer man revealed. He saw an unjust heart in the midst of a burning zeal for justice. That is what made his repentance so profound and complete.

Truth in the Innermost Being

We should be praying for God to send a few more Nathans, and not just to our neighbor whose hypocrisy we see so clearly. God desires truth in the innermost being and wisdom in the hidden parts. If it is not there, we are false, despite all of our outward professions. Truth is spirit; it has to do primarily with our spirit, our heart, and our innermost being. To walk in truth is to walk in and by the Spirit of Truth. Walking in the Spirit will mean speaking and thinking truly, never in opposition to our heart, but rather as expression and manifestation of our heart. That is what it means to walk in truth.

Does Christ live in us? We say that He does, and we tell others so, but others are unmoved and unimpressed. We can tell ourselves that this is a positional and judicial fact only and not an experiential one, but that explanation hardly satisfies us, let alone the skeptical non-Christians all around us.

Jesus did not say, "I am positionally the truth," nor did He say, "The truth has set you positionally free." We know that this is not the gospel. We know instinctively that truth by its very nature is more powerful than that. Lies don't make us positionally slaves: they make us experientially slaves, because they have the power of a spirit working within them. Truth must be at least as powerful as lies. Then why does it seem so weak and feeble?

Words, Power, and Full Conviction

Paul wrote to the Thessalonians,

> **Our gospel did not come to you in word only, but also in power and in the Holy Spirit and with full conviction; just as you know what kind of men we proved to be among you for your sake. (I Th 1:5 NAS).**

The apostle's words came in power because day by day his life was a demonstration of truth among those to whom he spoke. He *was* true, and so the true words he spoke had power and full conviction. To walk in God is to walk in truth, and others will experience Him in us only to the degree that we are actually walking in Him.

There is a story about what once happened when Charles Finney toured a textile mill in New York State. As he walked through the mill, he approached a woman operating a loom. As he came toward her, she stopped her work. As he came closer, she began to tremble. As he came still closer, she erupted in tears and finally fell to her knees and cried out to God for mercy; and Finney had not yet spoken a word. How often have we had just the opposite experience: hearing someone speak a multitude of words and not being moved at all? What accounts for the difference between a man who says nothing, yet brings a woman under conviction, and one who says much, yet leaves us unaffected? The answer lies, largely in part, if not entirely, in the fact that the truth is in us, and we in it, only to the degree that we actually walk in it.

CHAPTER 2

Truth that Transforms

Outward Form vs. Inward Reality

Seeing truth as a spirit to be walked in not only changes us individually, but also changes our whole understanding of what the Church is. When truth is seen as no more than a sum of truths to profess, the Church is seen as just a sum of individuals who all profess the same truths. That is why we consider the Church to be in the truth solely on the basis of the correctness or orthodoxy of its doctrinal statement. However, if truth is more than words and doctrines, then the Church, as much as its individual members, needs to *walk* in the truth in order to *be* in the truth.

The spiritual condition of the Church is not going to exceed the spiritual condition of its members. How can our relationships be any more real than we ourselves are? Christians are intended by God to be the most real people on earth. The Church ought, therefore, to be a haven and refuge from the hypocrisy and self-deceit of the world, the place to which truth-starved men and women can flee. What makes it such a haven is not any amount of words, but only people walking in truth, moment by moment, together.

The world is full of people with keen discernment, scrutinizing the Church. Our profession of truth has drawn all the more attention to ourselves. People in the world have learned to recognize pretense. They are well-schooled in the art of bluffing. They know all about convenience, expediency, insincerity, and manipulation. They can sense superficial relationships. If they find in the Church nothing essentially different from what is found outside of it, if they see no real difference in the way money and power are handled, then no amount of words, no matter how true they may be in themselves, is ever going to impress them.

A congregation, like an individual, can have an appearance of truth. It can stand upon the most orthodox and fundamental doctrines. It may have signs of blessing and prosperity in large numbers and abundant finances. It may even exhibit manifestations of spiritual gifts. But does it express truth in its innermost being? Or is it inwardly riddled with pretense and evasion, with shallow relationships, feigned love and unspoken animosities that subvert and contradict its words and make them, in effect, lies? God desires truth in the inward part. We need to begin to reckon truth as He does, which means according to our true spiritual condition and not our seeming, outward condition. It is the genuineness of our patience and forbearance and our commitment to speak and hear the truth in love that will reveal what we really are as the Church—not the volume and frequency of our "amens," "praise Gods," and "hallelujahs."

Love and Truth

The objection may be raised that too much is being made of truth when love is what is most crucial to us, both as individuals and as the Church. After all, didn't Jesus say, **"By this all men will know that you are My disciples, if you have love for one another"? (Jn 13:35 NAS).** Love is crucial, and sadly lacking, but the reason it is lacking has largely to do with how we conceive of love in relationship to truth.

The world is desperate for love and obsessed with seeking it. There is an incessant flood of talk about love in music, in literature, on television and radio talk shows, yet has the world ever been more vulgar, more violent, more sick and obscene than in our day? We are always in pursuit of love, but never able to find it. What men call love breaks down under pressure, degenerating into lifeless duty, or lust, or sentimentality. Real love has proven impossible for the world to achieve, and the reason why is not hard to discover. Jesus said,

> **I will ask the Father, and He will give you another Helper, that He may be with you forever; that is the Spirit of truth, Whom the world cannot receive, because it does not behold Him or know Him. (Jn 14:16-17 NAS).**

The world, by definition, cannot receive the Spirit of Truth. This is the very Spirit by which the love of God is shed abroad in our hearts. It is the very nature of the world to seek love apart from and at the cost of truth. It fervently seeks after love but cannot and will not receive truth; therefore, it finds neither truth nor love.

The world forfeits love when it turns away from truth. What then happens within the Church? Are we any more likely to find genuine love than those outside of the Church when we seek it apart from the Spirit of Truth?

John's second epistle begins,

> **The elder to the chosen lady and her children, whom I love in truth; and not only I, but also all who know the truth, for the sake of the truth which abides in us and will be with us forever: Grace, mercy and peace will be with us, from God the Father and from Jesus Christ, the Son of the Father, in truth and love. (II Jn 1-3 NAS).**

Four times in three verses the apostle of love, whose head rested upon Jesus' breast at their last meal together, mentions truth. Love and truth are so entwined, so permeated with each other that they are inseparable for John, and that is because they are inseparable for God. Therefore, they ought to be so for us. **"Whom I love in truth,"** John says. Is there any other way to love? If there were, we would have found it by now because we have tried so hard and for so long to discover it. Truth is threatening to us. We live in fear of truth, so we tend to structure our marriages and relationships and churches to insulate and protect us from it. Church, family and fellowship have evolved into elaborate systems for avoiding conflict and exposure and for skirting issues. The very architecture of most churches and our whole way of conducting services are perfectly suited to keeping any real involvement in the daily reality of each other's lives to an absolute minimum. Then, in our varying degrees of insulation, effectively cut off from any intimate contact with God or men, we cry out in desperation for love. What we get is false comfort, superficial healing, and some flimsy rationalizations and excuses. We give each other bear-hugs and say "God bless you" to one another, calling that love, and then go on pretending that all is well when all is not well. The gnawing hunger in our hearts persists. We begin by insulating ourselves from truth in order to protect ourselves; we end by insulating ourselves from love. Shielding ourselves from truth does not protect love; it suffocates it. The only thing preserved by being sheltered from truth is a lie.

Is there any significance in the fact that John, the disciple who spoke so much about truth, was also the one who rested his head on the bosom of the Lord? He even referred to himself as the disciple whom Jesus loved. Is there some connection? Did this affection shared between John and Jesus have anything to do with John's love of truth? John's head could finally come to rest upon Jesus' breast, the questionings could finally cease, and the fear and loneliness could dissolve. The bond of love was sealed and sure because there was nothing between them, no protective insulation, nothing pretended, nothing concealed. They were together in truth, and thus united in love. If we are casual with, or indifferent towards truth, if we still feign and pretend, then upon whose breast is our head going to lie?

We desperately need to put our heads to rest upon the bosom of the Lord, both individually and collectively. What prevents us? The answer does not lie so much in our theology as in our inability (or is it unwillingness?) to walk in truth. Perhaps we have been driven away by too much painful exposure to a cold, compassionless light masquerading as truth. We need to be reminded again that mercy and truth are met together (Ps 85:10); that the Spirit of Truth is the Comforter; that the sun of Righteousness always rises with healing in its wings (Mal 4:2). Truth, after all, is not the flat, dead glare of a police searchlight. It is not cold and lifeless; it is a spirit and a supreme mercy to all who welcome it and love it.

Purified Souls

The most overlooked and neglected remedy for lovelessness is a large dose of truthfulness. However, simply accumulating more truths will not produce more love. Truths are of no value unless they penetrate the heart and make us more true. Love can only exist in an atmosphere of truth. In any other atmosphere, regardless of what words are spoken, love must of necessity be feigned and false. It is a delusion and a lie to believe that we can love or be loved truly, while not living truly. Peter implied as much when he wrote, **"Seeing ye have purified your souls in obeying the truth through the**

Spirit unto unfeigned love of the brethren, see that ye love one another with a pure heart fervently." (I Pe 1:22 KJV). Unfeigned love requires first a purified soul. That includes, but is far more than, informed intellect. Only by obeying the truth by the Spirit, and not just the intellect, can we be purged of every false and deceptive thing, until what flows out from us is unfeigned love for one another. Until truth has gone this deep, it is vain to expect or require fervent love.

By this all men will know that we are Jesus' disciples, by the love we have for one another (Jn 13:34). Men will know because they will recognize a wholly different kind of love from what they have seen and known elsewhere, a love that is grounded in and issues from utter truth and reality. What we need to do is to frankly ask ourselves to what extent our love is in truth and to what degree it is no more than a correct doctrine or an outward sentiment. It is relatively easy for a white Christian to profess love for his black brother, until that brother moves in next-door or starts coming to church. It is relatively easy to pour out love and concern for Jews, until we encounter a Jew in real flesh, who draws all of our latent hatred and envy to the surface. We profess our love for each other and sing choruses about it in church, but the world outside is waiting to see what happens to our love when the trials and pressures of life put it to the test.

God is determined to bring us to love in truth or not at all. Either we are going to be a demonstration to the world of what real love is, or the world will not see real love. Feigned love is not going to suffice; only truth in the innermost being can result in unfeigned, fervent love of the brethren. So we are back to the issue of truth. Far from being an enemy or obstacle to love, truth proves to be the indispensable precondition for love. Real love does not evaporate in the light of truth. Real love *is* the light of truth. The only love that God's truth will dissipate is the love that is not God's. His fire will consume what is temporary and false, but it will purify and preserve what is lasting and true.

CHAPTER 3

Created to Live in Truth

The Most Practical and Urgent Necessity

With the Lord, walking in truth is not a luxury; it is the most practical and urgent necessity. Our spirits and our whole beings require truth in the same way that our bodies require air to breathe. We are made to live in truth, and when we do not, it is our whole beings that suffer. We can see the extent of the damage being done to our bodies by pollution in every aspect of the environment we live in. A continuous stream of impurity in everything we eat and drink and breathe constitutes an assault on every system of the body. The effect is the same when the pure spiritual atmosphere of truth is polluted with insincerity, guile, manipulation and deceit. And it only takes a little leaven to leaven a whole lump.

The whole human organism rebels against hypocrisy and lies. I may succeed in convincing myself that I am eating real food, at least enough to get my mouth to swallow it, but my body is wiser than my mouth. The digestive organs have no taste buds; their responses cannot be determined by how something tastes for the moment. They respond only to the real inner substance of what comes down to them, and they know, infallibly, whether it is true food or not. My innermost parts are just as honest in their response to insincerity and pretense. No matter how much I may tell myself that I am walking in truth, the inner parts cannot be deceived. The soul and spirit recoil from and rebel against a diet of untruth. Where do depression, anxiety, ulcers, and breakdowns come from? Are they completely unrelated to a life full of pretense and insincerity? Have they nothing at all to do with the wincing and contraction I feel far beneath my smile and mindless acknowledgment when someone tells me he loves me, and I know in my innermost part that he really does not? When I feign love, when I respond to a prayer as if sincere when I know it is not, or to a word of prophecy as if genuine when I know it is not, what effect does that have on my body and spirit? Every lie dulls the mind, confuses the emotions, and blunts the spirit of the one expressing it as well as the one receiving it, while adding to the unreality and untruth of the atmosphere we all breathe and depend upon for our lives together.

The world around us is cut off from the Spirit of Truth, and, as a result, it is choking to death on its own lies. Surely we would be fools to think that within the Church we could confine truth to our doctrines and still expect to live. We may be speaking truth, but even so, and in fact, all the more so, if we are not living it, then we will increasingly become the ravaged victims of the spirit of the lie.

The Leaven of Hypocrisy

When my way of comprehending truth changes, something else necessarily changes at the same time, and that is my way of perceiving the nature of untruth. If I see truth as only verbal and doctrinal, then I am sure to be seeing untruth as only verbal and doctrinal. The moment I realize that truth is a spirit that expresses itself in every area of life, the awareness comes also that untruth is, in essence, a spirit.

Jesus described the hypocrisy of the Pharisees as leaven for a very good reason. Hypocrisy is not merely an outer shell or mask over the surface of things, but an inner force intermixed with the whole substance of a life. When has a lump of dough only been leavened on its surface? The fact of the matter is that the outer surface may well be the last area to be affected. I can become a hypocrite even while the verbal surface of my life remains true, if my inner life becomes false. "Beware of the leaven of hypocrisy." Jesus' warning was aimed at the ever-present tendency to neglect truth in the inward parts and let the leaven, the spirit of the lie, corrupt one's walk. When that happens, the outer veneer of truth that remains becomes mask and a lie—the whitened sepulcher concealing a dead man's bones. And so, if I am not living truly, my speaking truths makes my condition worse, not better, because it hides the corruption beneath the surface until finally my words and doctrines themselves are corrupted from within and are transfigured into lies.

When Adam and Eve believed the serpent's lie in the garden, it was far more than their theology that was changed. The consequences of receiving that first lie into the heart of humanity have extended into every area of life, and even into nature itself. Every human institution has been leavened from within: politics, economics, psychology, religion, work, family. Nothing has escaped, although outward surfaces may retain every appearance of truth, objectivity and morality. The lie is a wolf that, by its very nature, always wears and very meticulously grooms sheep's clothing.

The Clash of Kingdoms

The clash of truth with untruth is not a verbal confrontation, not a cosmic debate to be won by the contestant who scores the most points in an argument. Rather, it is a clash of kingdoms, which are wholly opposed in ways of living, relating, conducting businesses, being wives and husbands, etc. True words alone cannot contend with the subtle and all-pervading spirit of untruth. In order to oppose the lies, Christians and the Church at large need to be true. The new humanity, the Church, needs to be as total an expression of truth as the old humanity is an expression of a lie. The Spirit of Truth is the distinctive of the believer, and of the Church of believers, as opposed to the world. It is, therefore, the distinctive of heaven as opposed to hell, of the new creation as opposed to the old, in the midst of which it has been placed.

What sort of evangelism follows from such a picture of truth in the midst of lies? From the beginning it manifested itself in the cry, **"Repent, for the kingdom of heaven is at hand!"** (Mt 3:2 NAS) and thousands were snatched out of the old and into the new creation. **"Be saved from this perverse generation,"** (Ac 2:40 NAS) Peter urged, and that is just what men did! What was the power and authority that caused those words to penetrate and break the grip of the lies and deception and darkness into which they were spoken? When men cried out, "Repent, for the Kingdom of God is at hand!" those hearing repented because the kingdom *was* at hand. There was a living declaration of it already present, a new Israel in which there was no guile. How much power is there going to be in my declaration, if in my life there remains guile and pretense and all the same manifestations of the spirit of the lie that captivates the world?

"Save yourselves from this perverse, twisted generation." Come out from a whole life, a whole humanity, a whole world that is being suffocated and devoured by unreality and lies. Come out of death and into life; out of lies and into clarity and truth; out of extortion and greed and into unfeigned love. This is the good news that the Church is commissioned to proclaim, but it is seldom sounded today, and when it is, it is most often lacking in penetrating power. Our evangelism is the projection of our Christian experience. When salvation has actually been a translation out of one creation into another, out of a kingdom of darkness into one of light, we can sense the difference. When salvation is being daily experienced as something far less than that, we can sense that alsoæregardless of the words that are employed.

If our evangelism has become shallow, then it is only because our Christianity has become shallow. If our evangelism has become mechanical and predictable, then more than likely so have our lives as believers. If our proclamation of the good news is merely verbal and formalized, then that is a sure sign that truth has become mere words and formulas in our daily walk. I cannot draw someone to a place I am not in myself. We can always *speak* the proclamation; to do so requires only that we remember the correct words. However, in order to move men, we need also to *be* the proclamation, and that requires a life immersed in the Spirit of Truth.

Jesus knew very well that right words alone were not enough. His followers already had all the right words when He commanded them to wait in Jerusalem for the power to turn those words into life

You shall receive power when the Holy Spirit has come upon you; and you shall be My witnesses both in Jerusalem, and in all Judea and Samaria, and even to the remotest part of the earth. (Ac 1:8 NAS).

What is the power to be a witness of Him? The Spirit came and gave the words to speak and the boldness to speak them and the miracles to confirm them, but being a witness entails more than being able to testify. We continually lapse into the mistaken notion that being a witness is something that we *do,* apart from something we *are.* This mistaken notion of ours follows from another more fundamental error, which is our belief that the Holy Spirit was sent to the Church on Pentecost as power, apart from His essential natureæthe Spirit of Truth.

While the Spirit did fall as power, He also came as the Spirit of Christ Himself, the very Spirit of Truth by which alone we can be a living demonstration, a witness of the truth. The power that the newborn Church was commanded to wait for was, and still is, the Spirit of Truth.

Being Right vs. Being Real

The world is suffering from its calculated indifference to truth. How are we going to bring it healing if we are indifferent to truth ourselves? As Christians, we can be very exacting about sin, as we ought to be, but we go on as if we did not consider pretense and guile to be sin as well. There has been too much pretending in Christendom, too much withholding of ourselves, too much putting on a brave face and whistling in the dark. We have for too long gone on saying the customary words while our hearts were out of tune with our professions. *We* have succeeded at being "right" but have failed at being real.

God has been very merciful and patient with us. He has a great compassion for our fears and weaknesses, but He has given us a power to be real, and He has the right to expect us to live by it. He has waited long for us, but we should not expect Him to wait forever. It is going to take a painful, fearful adjustment for many of us to begin to walk in truth, but what is the alternative? Our health requires it, our sanity demands it, and our very lives depend upon it, for a life that is not true is not life.

CHAPTER 4

The Holy Spirit of Truth

Truth Commanded...and Promised

It is a principle with God that when He requires something of us He also provides the means of fulfillment. Every commandment is at the same time a promise. **"Thou shalt love"** is the ultimate requirement and the summation of all of the law. To feel its full weight is to crumble in despair of ever fulfilling it. However, under the new covenant, this very same requirement is transformed into a promise that produces hope and life. "Thou shalt love." What is it that makes the difference? What transforms this requirement into a living hope? Paul called it a mystery, hidden throughout the ages, now revealed to us: Christ in us, the hope of glory (Col 1:27).

My experience with a commandment of God is what determines how I will experience His provision for fulfilling it. The hope of glory will continue to be a veiled mystery to me as long as I conceive of my goal as well, as God's intention, as something less than glory. The apostle Paul was a man who had lived with the law for his whole life and was quite satisfied that he had been fulfilling it. He was a Hebrew of the Hebrews, a Pharisee, holding to the strictest and most scrupulous interpretation of God's requirements. As far as the righteousness of the law was concerned, he described himself as blameless (Phil 3:5-6). Then something happened. **"When the commandment came...I died." (Ro 7:9).** I thought I had comprehended its requirement. I thought that the measure of provision I had was sufficient to fulfill it, but then the law fully came. The extent of what it required was suddenly unveiled, and I saw how far it exceeded my ability to ever attain it. Unless a greater provision for fulfillment can be found, there is no hope.

This is exactly our situation when we come face to face with the divine requirement to walk in truth. **"Each of you must put off falsehood and speak truthfully to his neighbor." (Eph 4:25 NIV).** We never realized what was being demanded of us. We never imagined that this meant something more than abstaining from conspicuously speaking lies to one another. Then the commandment fully came, and we saw how deep and subtle falsehood was. We experienced God's requirement, penetrating to the innermost parts of our being and extending to every aspect of our lives. Truth, like righteousness, is far more than we thought it was. In fact, *everything* about God is far more than we thought it was. How, then, are we going to be able to walk in truth? The veil has been pulled back, and the full meaning of the commandment has been revealed, while at the same time a whole new depth of meaning to a divine promise has been revealed. **"I will pray to the Father, and He shall give you another Comforter...even the Spirit of Truth...He will guide you into all truth." (Jn 14:16-17, 16:13).** What a requirement! What a promise! What a provision!

Jesus said, **"It is expedient for you that I go away." (Jn 16:7).** How many of us really believe that? Have you ever wished He were present in the flesh, that you could see Him and talk with Him just as the first disciples did? If we were honest, we would probably say that it would be very expedient if He had remained and ruled and judged as a king on the earth. He could have objectively answered every theological question, settled every debate, conclusively proved how right we and our denomination (or non-denomination) really are. In fact, in our candor, we might even suggest that departing was the least expedient thing He could have done. He left us His Word, but He did not leave us anyone to say whose interpretation of it is the right one. How is it expedient for us that He went away?

The Holy Spirit is the Spirit of Truth

Until His commandment strikes home, until His intention for us dawns upon our hearts, it will not be expedient for us that He has gone. While I see truth as essentially consisting of doctrines and theologies, my greatest need is for an objective, external Christ to objectively decide for me between truth and error. The same is true of the man who still believes that righteousness consists essentially in doing the right thing. For him, the most useful provision God could make would be an elaborately detailed statement of law, applying it to every possible situation. It is only when my comprehension of truth and righteousness is radically broadened and deepened that I begin to agree with Jesus that it is good that He departed. **"It is expedient for you that I go away...if I go...the Comforter...will...come unto you." (Jn 16:7 KJV).** For the man who sees that truth is something to be in the innermost part, the only provision that could possibly meet his profound need is the very Spirit of Truth within. Our need for holiness, for power, and for comfort, all point to one provision: Christ in us, the hope of glory. What seems tragically to escape our notice is that this Christ in us, this Comforter, this Spirit of Holiness and Power is the Spirit of Truth. The Spirit that fell on Pentecost was and still is the Spirit of Truth.

Jesse Penn-Lewis, observed that, "The name 'Comforter' depicts His (the Spirit's) work, but His name the 'Spirit of

Truth' describes His essential character; therefore, all that He does in and for men as the 'Comforter' He must do in accordance with His character as the Spirit of Truth." (Jessie Penn-Lewis, *The Spirit of Truth,* Page 4, Overcomers Literature Trust, 3 Munster Rd., Parkstone, Pool, Dorset, England).

Whatever God's Spirit does in terms of comfort, empowerment, counsel, and encourage, He can do only as the Spirit of Truth. If we are indifferent or resistant toward truth, it is not only truth that we will lack, but everything that the Spirit of Truth was intended to convey. It is vain to expect Him to come to us as comfort when He is being rejected as truth. God cannot give false comfort. God cannot feign love. Everything He does is an expression of who He is, and He must be true to Himself. The Spirit is the Spirit of Truth because God is the God of Truth.

If I am receiving a comfort that sidesteps truth, I need to seriously question the nature and source of that comfort. My need for consolation in affliction and suffering is very real, but my need for truth is always as great, if not greater. It is no mercy to allow someone to continue in illusions and lies. I may desire such a mercy, but God loves me too much to extend it. His comfort always comes with truth. It is the truth that keeps comfort from becoming fuel for my self-pity. It is the truth that keeps power from feeding my pride and lust for glory. In the end, according to Paul the apostle, men perish not because they would not receive a love of power or a love of comfort, but **"because they refused to love the truth and so be saved." (II Th 2:10 NIV).**

Desiring the Guileless Transparency of Jesus

To love truth is to desire the guileless transparency of Jesus more than anything else. It needs to be a very powerful desire, because along with that transparency comes some things we may very strongly want to escape and refuse. Receiving a love for truth, and the Spirit who is truth, means facing the prospect of life without recourse to exaggeration or "white" lies or flattery, or anything I have grown accustomed to employing in order to enlarge or to protect myself. It means playing no roles, assuming no poses. That, frankly, frightens most of us. The Spirit of Truth is going to lead us into all truth, even the parts that may humiliate us before men, leave us painfully uncertain and perplexed, and shatter our false images of ourselves, others, and ultimately of God Himself. That may not be what we were hoping for. We were looking for something far more quiet and safe and much less costly. Receiving the love of truth and the Spirit who leads us into all truth inevitably means a measure of suffering, because disillusionment, uncertainty and humility are all forms of suffering—and suffering is what I desperately want to avoid! I will avoid it at all cost, even at the cost of truth itself, unless I love truth even more than I fear it. It is not ignorance that keeps us from becoming true; it is cowardice.

> **He who overcomes shall inherit these things, and I will be his God and he will be My son. But for the cowardly and unbelieving and abominable and murderers and immoral persons and sorcerers and idolaters and all liars, their part will be in the lake that burns with fire and brimstone, which is the second death. (Rev 21:7-8 NAS).**

Love of Truth Casts Out All Fear

The cowardly and the unbelieving are spoken of in one breath because at the heart of cowardice is a refusal to believe and trust God, who calls us to walk in truth. Truth is the only atmosphere in which faith and sanity can thrive and in which true comfort can be found. God never hides the fact that truth is at times painful to experience, just as He Himself is. On the other hand, He gives us every reason to love and trust truth, just as He gives us every reason to love and trust Himself. When I hesitate and withhold my trust, I am implying that a measure of shadow and pretense is necessary if I am to survive. I, in effect, declare that the Comforter is unable to comfort me in the undiluted light of truth and that God needs to evade His own nature in order to console me. Few ever let such thoughts become conscious, but conscious or not, once formed and inwardly affirmed, they make me a coward and an unbeliever, a lover of shadows and lies.

I begin a coward, and I end an idolater. If God is truth, if the Spirit of Truth is His Spirit, then who am I worshipping if I refuse to love and walk in the Spirit of Truth? Many will be there on that day when all illusions and shadows are removed by the full presence of Jesus, and they will protest that they performed many great works and preached many doctrinally correct sermons in His name. He will not deny their claims; He will only say, "I never knew you." You were never vitally joined with Me. You never loved My Spirit. You dreaded truth and never loved it or Me.

Our cowardice keeps us from the comfort we desperately need. We spare ourselves the pain of truth, but it is a pain attended by an altogether unique and healing comfort. **"I have many more things to say to you, but you cannot bear them now. But when He, the Spirit of truth, comes, He will**

guide you into all the truth." (Jn 16:12-13 NAS). He is also a comforter, and He alone can make all truth bearable. Without the Spirit of Truth, we are left with only a false comfort. False comfort is a way around suffering. True comfort is the way through it. False comfort can never lead to the Father because it is, after all, an expression of untruth, just as true comfort is an expression of truth itself. False comfort, like false anything, leads only to bondage, not freedom; it leads to the father of lies, not the Father of Light.

We can refuse to love truth. Such a refusal does not consist of a singular, all-at-once act. It is, rather, the cumulative effect of a lifetime of choosing lies and half-truths, of preferring comfort over truth, of preferring a safe and painless way above the leading of the Spirit. When the Spirit comes to lead us out of an illusion, out of half-truth and into the whole truth, what is our response? Do we prefer the security of the convenient and familiar? Do we cling to the partial knowledge that has served us so well? Or do we welcome Him and in obedience, however costly, follow Him where we would never care, or dare, to go ourselves; that is, into all truth? It is how we walk daily that makes us either lovers of truth or cowards in flight from it.

CHAPTER 5

Truth in Character and Conduct

The Lowly Jordan

Invitations to the mountaintop are very popular. Invitations to the Jordan, however, are seldom sought after. If someone is seeking after the Spirit of Truth, it is in the valley, not on the mountaintop, that he finds what he is looking for. Jesus knew that He required the Spirit in perfect fullness in order to accomplish all that was set before Him. He knew that the way of the Lord prepared for Him was John's baptism and the stark humility that it signified. For Him, though He spoke with Elijah himself on the mountaintop, John was 'Elijah' down in the valley. **"If you are willing to accept it," Jesus said, "he [John] is the Elijah who was to come." (Mt 11:14 NIV).** If you have an unquenchable longing to see the Lord's way prepared in your own life, if you desire truth in the innermost parts, if you desire to stand before the Pilates of this age as living expressions of truth, then John will be to you Elijah. Those who desire less than the Spirit without measure will not perceive John as Elijah, nor will they perceive the lowly Jordan as the place where the Spirit must be found. But if this lowly place was where the sinless Son of God had to begin, then how can we imagine it possible for us to begin anywhere else or any other way?

John attracted some large crowds. Many came out from Jerusalem to see him. Some were merely curious. Some were just gathering notes for seminary research papers on repentance or for next Sunday's sermon. The ones who were there looking for truth were the ones who came, left everything false behind, and walked out into the water to be baptized. That kind of repentance is the fruit and the sign of a longing after truth and the God of truth. Until we have resolved to walk in truth, free from all deception, we will remain back in our own Jerusalem, or we will come to see John out of curiosity, not truly perceiving him at all. But once that resolve is made, it inevitably leads beyond the banks and into the waters of the Jordan.

Truth: The Character of Christ in Us

The first step down to the place where the Spirit descends upon human flesh is the realization of our great need and the birth of a pure, holy hatred for our own pretenses and hypocrisies. Such longing after truth and such a hatred of all forms of the lie is the stirring of the character of the Son of God in us. It is upon that character alone that the dove from heaven descends and abides. It instinctively recognizes an identity, a kinship with the character of Christ. Upon such a character and in such a humble place, the Spirit can come down in His fullness and express not just His attributes and gifts, but His very nature and essence, which is truth.

At the same time that the heavens opened and the Spirit of God descended as a dove and alighted on Jesus, the voice of God sounded from heaven, **"This is my beloved Son, in whom I am well pleased." (Mt 3:17 NAS).** The Father chose this moment to declare His pleasure. His expression of pleasure did not come because of anything that Jesus had done.

Jesus had not yet done anything; His ministry, as such, had not yet begun. God's greatest joy, like John's, is to see His children walking in truth. The Father's pleasure was, and is, in His Son's character, in what He *is*, above and before what He *does*. All that Jesus did, all the authority that He had, flowed from who He was. Even if it were possible to duplicate or even exceed Jesus' deeds, it would remain impossible to gain His authority or to know the Father's joy in any way other than by walking in truth as His beloved Son.

God reserved His Spirit and His audible voice of approval for the moment of Jesus' baptism; He reserved the revelation of His Son's identity to John for that moment as well. Jesus' identity was so bound up with the Spirit of Truth that the Baptist was not permitted to recognize him by anything else, even though as a blood relative, none had greater reason to know Him in the flesh.

> **And I did not recognize Him, but in order that He might be manifested to Israel, I came baptizing in water...And I did not recognize Him, but He who sent me to baptize in water said to me, 'He upon whom you see the Spirit descending and remaining upon Him, this is the one...' And I have seen, and have borne witness that this is the Son of God.**
>
> **(Jn 1:31-34 NAS).**

Jesus was likely no stranger to John. Their mothers were cousins. They may have grown up not far from each other. John was most probably in a position to observe Jesus. Yet, nothing natural in itself counted as a sign of who Jesus was. Being a close relation was of no help to John, and God did not designate any miraculous works as definitive signs of who Jesus was. The works later confirmed what only character could reveal. It was the coming down, and not just that, but the abiding of the Spirit, that constituted God's chosen sign to John that Jesus was the expected Messiah. What John witnessed was not a momentary conjunction, not a passing touch of the Spirit to meet a moment's need, but a lasting union, a unity of essence and character.

It was not enough for John to see the Spirit touch Jesus, just as it is not enough for our contemporaries to see the Spirit occasionally touch the Church today. What John saw was the Spirit descending and abiding on human flesh. He saw the Holy Spirit, the Spirit of Truth, so at one with a man's character that He could remain and reside with him. The skeptics and the seekers who observe the conduct of Christians need to see the same thing.

Humility and Repentance

John said that he came baptizing in order that Jesus might be made manifest to Israel. Israel needed to be to repent and be baptized in order to be able to see their Messiah, but John also baptized Jesus Himself. Was it any less essential that Jesus be baptized in order for Him to be made manifest? We wait for those "stubborn Jews" to finally see the true meaning of all the Old Testament messianic prophecies and to succumb, along with the Gentile world, to our evangelistic programs. However, perhaps Jews and Gentiles and God Himself have been waiting for us to be made manifest as children of God who walk in truth. We have been content in our Christian "Jerusalem" to point to all sorts of signs as proof of a living Christ.

For the most part, the world, and most especially Israel, has not been convinced. We are waiting for them to somehow be induced to enter into the waters of humility and repentance in order to be able to recognize our Christ and His Church, but perhaps Israel has come only as far as the banks of the Jordan, and their salvation awaits *our* entrance into the water, as Jesus Himself entered. Israel, along with the rest of the skeptical world, needs first to see the Church made manifest, stripping off its pomp and pretense, coming down out of its high places to the lowly valley of the Jordan, submitting to a washing in humility and repentance. When Israel and the world can see the Spirit of Truth descend and abide upon the Church and hear the Father say to the Church, **"This is My beloved Son in whom I am well pleased; I have no greater joy than this, to hear of my children walking in the truth,"** **(Mt 3:17; III Jn 4)** perhaps then they will be induced to enter the waters of repentance themselves and to believe.

The Patience of the Dove

The baptism of Jesus was not the first example in Scripture of a dove finding an earthly place in which to abide. The very earth itself was submerged in a watery tomb in Noah's day. After the rain had ceased, Noah released two birds from the ark. One was a raven. It never returned. Though the floodwater had not receded, the raven was apparently content to land upon any remnant of the old, judged earth that might happen to float. The other bird returned to the ark. Unlike the raven, it found no place to rest its feet. It was a far more particular kind of bird. "Just anything" would not do. It required a place in keeping with its own impeccable character. It was a dove. Only after the floodwater receded and a renewed earth emerged did that dove find a place to abide.

That dove must have had extraordinary patience. After being so long in the ark, it must have longed to live again unconfined. Yet, it would not seize the first opportunity it had to roost in any old thing. How long was the Spirit from heaven waiting patiently for the coming of Jesus? Has the character of the dove changed since Noah's day? Has He become less patient and less particular? Has He become so weary of circling over the remains of our old humanity that He has finally contented Himself to take up residence with anything that floats? His character has not changed. The presence of gifts and manifestations with us is not proof to the contrary. The dove may graciously touch and give gifts, apparently indiscriminately, but He remains very discriminating when it comes to finding a place to fully abide, so as to express His character.

Noah required great patience as well. The storm was over and the sun was shining again. After more than seven months of confinement, the ark came to rest on a mountaintop, and Noah had waited. God was the One who closed the door to the ark, but it was Noah's decision when to open it. He let the dove be his sign that the time had come. In a sense, Noah had no choice but to wait for dry land to appear. For us, the choice is harder. We are saved and baptized. Why wait any longer? Why submit to yet more restraint and limitation? Can't we assume that God will bless whatever we do, however we do it?

Truth's Lovers Wait

Our impatience is our undoing and the revelation of our heart. The problems and needs that surround us are too great, too pressing. Our personal lives, our families, our churches cry out for solutions, for something that will work to produce a measure of order and stability. There are financial pressures, there is a world to evangelize, there is a marriage to salvage, there is a watching world needing to be impressed that this

Christianity we profess is genuine. Under such circumstances, who could wait? Is it really so wrong to pretend or exaggerate just a little bit, to grab hold of some of the old proven ways and devices that worked so well in the past and still work in the world around us?

In fact, wouldn't it be "super-spiritual" and irresponsible to wait any longer? The only thing that will induce us to wait, the only thing that can restrain us from stepping out of the ark and taking hold of some floating residue of our old humanity, is an impassioned love for truth and a hatred of everything tainted by lies. Without such an inner restraint, we will be quick to grasp what we can, willing to feign feelings and manipulate others. And when we do, it is not the dove that we will find abiding there with us, but a much less patient, much less particular "bird"!

One whole book of the New Testament is devoted to the Acts of the Apostles, but, interestingly, the Book of Acts begins in complete inactivity. The Cross is history, Jesus is resurrected, and the disciples have come to believe in Him, yet Luke writes that, **"Gathering them together, He commanded them not to leave Jerusalem, but to wait." (Ac 1:4 NAS)**. Waiting is never easy. It is a form of suffering, and it is all the more acute when one is surrounded by danger and need. Yet, after three years of the most intense, personal experience with Jesus and after forty days of instruction on the kingdom from the risen Lord, here they were required to wait. Jesus was convinced that the task before them was too great to be fulfilled on the basis of their knowledge and experience. They were told to wait for power, not so much to "do witnessing" as to be witnesses (Ac 1:8). The requirement to *be* is always far greater and more demanding than the requirement to *do*!

The number of days that Jesus instructed His disciples about the kingdom is the same as the number of days it rained while Noah was in the ark. Perhaps hearing about the kingdom directly from Jesus is less like a school than a baptism, in which all of our known conceptions of the kingdom, the Church, and our witness are washed over and purged. If we could experience that sort of instruction, we would be much more disposed to wait; we would be unable to do anything but wait for power from above.

It is Not for You to Know

What did Jesus teach during those forty days? If only Luke had recorded at least some of His words, we might have the answers to some of the perplexing questions that believers have asked ever since. But Luke tells us nothing more; he only records the questions that the disciples asked after Jesus was finished teaching them and Jesus' responses to those questions. **"Is it at this time You are restoring the kingdom to Israel?" (Ac 1:6 NAS).** We can easily put ourselves in their place: What about the rapture, Lord? When exactly is the tribulation? What exactly does "all Israel shall be saved" mean? Are these the Last Days? We all want to know, and there is nothing wrong with a concern for such questions. But of still greater concern is Jesus' answer to the disciples: **"It is not for you to know...but you shall receive power when the Holy Spirit has come upon you; and you shall be My witnesses." (Ac 1:7-8 NAS).** Knowledge is not primary. Receiving power to be witnesses of Him is not dependent upon the "how" and "when" of the kingdom. I do not have to first know all the truths, but I do have to be true.

"It is not for you to know" can be very hard to take for an answer, especially when you think you already know. What terrible irony it is that our knowledge, even, and especially about end time and kingdom things, can be the greatest obstacle to becoming witnesses of Him. "Not knowing" may well be a necessary condition for being the living instruments that God can use to bring His purposes to pass. Not knowing frees a man from the self-consciousness of his place and role that can cripple him spiritually. Not knowing is a divine antidote to the poison of spiritual pride. Knowledge of end time truths and kingdom principles can ironically make a person less true; it can render one's vocabulary stilted, hollow, and predictable; it can eclipse the very spontaneity and childlikeness of spirit that the reality of the kingdom requires. Hearing Jesus say, "it is not for you to know" has the power to bring even the greatest of disciples to a halt. Pentecost was never intended to empower us to bear witness to our knowledge. It was intended to empower us to be witnesses of Him.

The path to the upper room, like the one Jesus followed to the Jordan, led down, not up. The men left waiting that last ten days in Jerusalem had all been brought low, profoundly humbled. Every one of them could recall the still recent experience of having denied Jesus. They had all said they were prepared to die with Him, and they had all had their own illusions about themselves shattered. By the time they reached the upper room, they were reduced to truth and hence were prepared to receive the Spirit of Truth in full measure and in His deepest self-revelation. Pentecost would have made them only "Pentecostals," witnesses *of* Pentecost, but not witnesses *of* Jesus, if they had not first walked a path down, as to the Jordan, to get to the upper room.

In Israel's history, profound transitions occurred when the Israelites passed through bodies of water. Israel entered Canaan by crossing the Jordan and left Egypt by crossing through the Red Sea. The departure from Egypt was so abrupt, so total, that they could not even bring leaven along for their bread. A Christian's baptism marks at least as great a transition. It is an exodus from the old world through water, and it ought to be just as total and incisive. One very good measure of just how profoundly radical a transition redemption has been in our lives is to sample the bread we are feeding each other and ourselves. Was our passage through the waters of baptism so casual and indifferent as to permit us to bring along some leaven for our bread?

Leaven Renders Truth a Lie

Before we boast too quickly about our redemption and the gifts of the Spirit in our midst, we ought to consider Paul's words to the believers in Corinth:

> **Your boasting is not good. Do you not know that a little leaven leavens the whole lump of dough? Clean out the old leaven, that you may be a new lump, just as you are in fact unleavened. For Christ our Passover also has been sacrificed. Let us therefore celebrate the feast, not with old leaven...but with the unleavened bread of sincerity and truth. (I Cor 5:6-8 NAS).**

If the bread of our feast, the bread of our fellowship and service and worship, still contains the leaven of pretense, of feigned love, and of insincerity, then in what are we boasting? At issue is not the quantity of leaven, but its very presence. It only takes a little leaven to leaven the whole lump. It only takes a little pretense, a little simulation, to render the whole loaf of our relationships and our worship a lie. How abrupt and how total has our redemption been if we have had the time and inclination to bring some of the old leaven along with us?

"Clean out the old leaven," Paul said. All the leaven in Israel had to be purged before they could celebrate the feast of their redemption. The feast cannot be celebrated with leavened bread—only with the unleavened bread of sincerity and truth. We might be able to simulate the feast, to perform it correctly, but it is impossible to truly celebrate our redemption and our Redeemer in the absence of sincerity and truth.

The Leaven of Pretense and Insincerity

If, even after crossing through the waters of our own baptism, our bread is still leavened with pretense and insincerity, then it is fair and necessary to ask ourselves to what degree the heavenly dove still abides with us. How much of our spiritual gifts, raised hands and religious activity have ceased to be a living expression of the Spirit and become, instead, a form of leaven, a substitute for a grieved dove that has had to retract and withdraw? A little leaven leavens the whole lump! Lies cannot be quarantined. Feigned love for a brother leads to feigned worship towards God. And the dove from heaven cannot abide where lies abound. In the absence of that dove, we are forced to find some alternative, to imitate and pretend, and thereby spread the leaven and drive the Spirit into an ever-smaller recess in our lives. If we have found a way to go on and maintain an appearance of the Spirit, then that is not to our credit; rather, it is a sign of our failure and shame. We certainly are not fooling God. If we would stop and consider, we would be forced to admit that we really are not even fooling ourselves.

The Cost of Purging the Old Leaven

Purging the old leaven is going to be painful and costly. It means leaving everything that has "worked" behind, including the mere truce that has substituted for genuine peace in our relationships, the bluff and bravado that has served in place of genuine authority. Our personal lives and the history of the Church contain ample evidence of alternatives to truth that "works," but if it "works" and isn't true, then it is worthless. In fact, it is worse than worthless, because it makes us untrue and because we are inevitably going to collide with reality, so that what merely "worked" will all the more devastatingly fail. It may be a fearful prospect to face our spouses, our children, our congregations, and ourselves without the habitual and convenient lies that have "worked" for so long. Conversely, the prospect of facing reality armed only with lies, having our bluff called at a time when the stakes are real and ultimate, is even more fearful.

A baptism through which leaven can be successfully brought is very suspect. There is something about a thorough baptism that makes a mess of the best hairdos and takes the crease out of our Sunday-best pants. Everything on the surface of our lives, everything that constitutes mere appearance, suffers a mortal blow in the waters of baptism. Passing from the merely verbal to the real is just such a baptism, but it is when one comes up from these waters that one hears the voice of the Father and sees the Spirit descending and abiding!

From Fullness to Power

Immediately after His baptism, Jesus was tempted in the wilderness. One would think that this would be the least opportune time to test a man. Paradoxically, however, it was the very presence of the dove that made the temptation so timely and powerful in Jesus' life. According to Scripture, Jesus entered the wilderness in the fulness of the Spirit. Scripture also says not that Satan lured Him, but that the very Spirit that had just come upon Him in the Jordan had led Him there (Mt 4:1). The first consequence of being filled with the Spirit was not what we would expect. We would have Jesus come up out of the water and go straight to Jerusalem to proclaim the gospel in great power. Instead, according to Luke, the Spirit led Him into a barren place, alone, to become exhausted of all natural strength, and hungry after forty days of fasting. The Spirit Himself seems to have engineered a set of circumstances that invite temptation, which make it more, not less, appealing, and which make a man more, not less, vulnerable. Why?

The answer lies, at least in part, in God's supreme confidence in His Spirit. The Spirit abiding without limit in a vessel that is true can enable a man to withstand even ultimate temptation. That is how confident God is. How confident are we? How confident am I in the power of truth simply as truth, unaided by favorable circumstances, unsupported by natural strength, to reveal and overcome the most subtle of lies, especially when they come to me at a time when I most need the comfort and power that they offer? What kind of truth and what kind of relationship to it can engender the confidence and supply the spiritual stamina to withstand lies under such extreme conditions of temptation? Mere verbal truth will not sustain me under that sort of pressure, and if it cannot sustain me in the wilderness, then it will not be able to empower me back in Galilee and in Jerusalem when I go to proclaim and demonstrate the gospel. Jesus was led into the wilderness in the fullness of the Spirit (Lk 4:1). He came out of the wilderness and went into Galilee in the power of the

Spirit (Lk 4:14). If there is no fullness going into temptation, then there will be no power coming out of it.

Every need and desire that comes to us, both natural and spiritual, brings with it a temptation to resort to a lie, in order to fulfill it. More often than not, the temptation will come when we are in lonely, barren places, weak and vulnerable. If when temptation comes it finds pride, pretense, compromise, and play-acting in us, it will penetrate our merely verbal defenses and leave us without any real power when we go into Galilee. But if we have just come from the Jordan and have the Spirit abiding in fullness and have the quiet, unshakable assurance of our Father's pleasure, then temptation will work like a catalyst in us, transforming fulness into power. The power of the Spirit becomes a reality in us to the degree that every other false source of power has been resisted and rejected.

Test of Truth: Among Those Who Know Us

And Jesus returned to Galilee in the power of the Spirit...and He came to Nazareth, where He had been brought up. (Lk 4:14,16 NAS).

Nazareth is the last place we would go, unless we were certain of the power of the Spirit. Galilee and Nazareth are significant because they are "where He had been brought up." Jesus went directly to the people who knew Him. The greatest test is always at our doorstep, among those who know our every weakness and blemish, who see us walking out our faith daily. It is easier to bluff and deceive both others and ourselves where we are not known, where no one can look at us and say, "Isn't this Joseph the carpenter's son?" To begin, each of us in his own Nazareth, in his own family and fellowship and workplace, is another matter entirely.

And He came to Nazareth, where He had been brought up; and as was His custom, He entered the synagogue on the Sabbath, and stood up to read. And the book of the prophet Isaiah was handed to Him. And He opened the book, and found the place where it was written, "The Spirit of the Lord is upon Me, because He anointed Me to preach the gospel to the poor. He has sent Me to proclaim release to the captives, and recovery of sight to the blind, to set free those who are downtrodden, to proclaim the favorable year of the Lord. (Luke 4:16-18 NAS).

Bluffing vs. Substance

It would be foolhardy for us to go into our own Nazareths today and proclaim that the Lord has anointed us to heal the brokenhearted and set the captives free without the heavenly dove abiding with us in fullness and power as He did with Jesus. **"And He closed the book...and sat down; and the eyes of all in the synagogue were fixed upon Him." (Lk 4:20 NAS).** So also will the eyes of everyone be upon us when they hear like words coming from our mouths! If we are bluffing by merely mouthing words without the substance behind them, we would do better to not call so much attention to ourselves. The world has grown used to hearing the words and dismissing those who speak them. One penetrating glance is sufficient to reveal that the speaker need not be taken seriously.

When Jesus sat down and everyone fixed his gaze on Him, He did not qualify His words or contrive a strategic verbal retreat. They were calling His bluff, testing His substance. His response was to say, **"Today this Scripture has been fulfilled in your hearing." (Lk 4:21 NAS).**

The broken and captive inhabitants of today's Nazareths are waiting to hear such words again. They need to turn and fix their cynical gaze on the Church and say, not with scorn, but with surprised astonishment, "Isn't this Joseph's son? Aren't these those same Christians who are always riddled with inconsistencies, full of platitudes, and captive to the same greeds and fears as we are? Then what is this fervency of love, this transparency, simplicity and clarity, this evident reality?" May the day come when what was said about Jesus will be said about His Church: **"And they were amazed at His teaching, for His message was with authority."** (Lk 4:32 NAS).

That day needs to come, because there is another day coming when the illusions that men cleave to for a semblance of security and sanity will crumble and dissolve. If men were leaping from windows when the economy staggered into depression in 1929, what will happen to our far softer, more pampered generation when the whole present world system begins to totter and collapse? Everything that can be shaken will be shaken. Everything founded upon illusions and half-truths and pride and greed and fear will ultimately collide with reality. There will be many more downtrodden and brokenhearted, many more captive and blind and bewildered then. Will the Church be the only remaining source of sanity to turn to and cling to, or will it be as desolate and distraught as the world, suddenly bereft of the same lies and illusions?

When Jesus read from Isaiah He stopped in the middle of a verse. He concluded, **"to proclaim the favorable year of the Lord."** That last verse ends, **"and the day of vengeance of our God."** (Is. 61:2 NAS). We are destined to complete that verse. The world has grown accustomed to the sight of strange men on street corners carrying doomsday placards declaring, "Repent, for the end of the world is at hand!" When the Church is not taken seriously, those who proclaim a coming judgment are taken as fools. That is because men do not see that day coming. They are blind to the pre-dawn light of that day, a light that even now illumines and reveals everything in the world as vanity and lies. The failure to see a lie as a lie has nothing to do with faulty eyesight. A lie is not seen as a lie precisely because it is believed, because too much security and comfort and power is derived from it for the one believing it to allow its delusive nature to be recognized.

The ability to see a lie as a lie has nothing to do with mere verbal understanding of the doctrine of final judgment. The ability to see a lie as a lie comes from not believing it, from rejecting and refusing the security and comfort and power that the lie offers. Do we see biblically and experience the whole world as begotten of a lie? If we do not, then we are as blind as unbelievers, despite our correct words about eschatology. And if those who are leading the blind and preaching the gospel to them and offering them sight are themselves blind, then they can only ultimately fall together into the same ditch.

Judgment: To The Church First

There is a reason why judgment, not just the doctrine of judgment, needs to come first to the Church. The Church needs to have the light of truth shined on its own lies and illusions. It needs to have everything founded on unreality and nurtured in shadows brought crashing down. It needs to see everything in the light, everything, including itself, as it really is, just as God sees it. The light of truth is judgment to everything that is not true. The Church, in so far as it is true, is living in and radiating the light of the day of judgment even now in the midst of the world. Only such a Church, and such believers, already a living proclamation of the soon-coming day of God's judgment, can proclaim the healing of the broken-hearted and the restoring of sight to the blind.

The light of God's truth changes more than a man's doctrines; it changes the man. Isaiah was already a great prophet, but in the year that King Uzziah died, Isaiah saw something that transformed him. Isaiah saw the Lord in His glory, and the result of that vision was not a treatise or an interesting series of sermons. Isaiah fell as a dead man and cried out that he was a man of unclean lips and that he dwelt among a people of unclean lips. **"Woe is me, I am undone!"** he cried. **(Isaiah 6:5).** He saw as God sees. He saw everything as it really was, and he was undone. Only afterwards could he go and proclaim the words that Jesus read in the synagogue at Nazareth, words of hope and healing, because he was healed and restored; he could speak words of judgment and wrath because he himself had been purged and judged.

Are we going to be commissioned and anointed to proclaim and perform what Isaiah did while our lips are still unclean with the taint of half-truths and insincerity? Are we going to do greater works than Jesus did by a power less than He had? We may be able to speak about a soon-coming day of judgment, but if we are not already walking in the light of that day, then our words are a mockery of that truth.

Our Deepest Longing and Goal

We are already sons of God, but we do not yet know what we shall be. We do not yet know what it is to be completely like Him (I Jn 3:2,3), but such a complete likeness is, or at least ought to be, our deepest longing and our goal. We do know that when He comes, we will be like Him, because then we shall see Him as He really is, not clouded by our illusions, fears and desires. If this is one's hope, he will purify himself, even as He is pure. The Church that lives in and by this hope will be purifying itself, speaking truth to one another in love, restoring one another's sight, keeping one another true.

Such a process, always loving, is often painful. The love of truth may require some extreme acts. The day that God consecrated the Levites for His service was the day Moses came down from the mount and found all Israel in debauchery and idolatry. He said, **"Whoever is for the Lord, come to me!" (Ex 32:26 NAS)**. A small remnant came and joined him. They had to make a choice as whether to eat and drink and rise up and play, or to follow the Lord, whether to indulge in the consolations of lies, or entrust themselves to truth. To those who joined him, Moses said, **"Every man of you put his sword upon his thigh, and go...in the camp, and kill every man his brother...friend, and...neighbor." (Ex 32:27 NAS)**. How much do we love the truth? Do we love it enough to ruthlessly put on the sword and go in and out of the camp, enough to go in and out of our own homes, our own marriages, our own congregations, and our own thought life, to slay everything untrue? Any lesser love is unpriestly.

> **Therefore, rejecting all falsity...let every one express the truth with his neighbor, for we are all parts of one body and members one of another... For once you were darkness, but now you are light in the Lord; walk as children of light...for the fruit...of the Light...[consists] in every form of kindly goodness, uprightness of heart and trueness of life. (Eph 4:25,5:8-9 Amplified).**

Trueness of life is the result and the evidence of rejecting all falsity in all of its forms. Like every fruit, it is not something that can be attained by our own striving. Trueness of life can only be produced by the Spirit, whose own essential nature is truth. The way of knowing a tree has not changed. It always has been and always will be by its fruit. If the Spirit of Truth is the sap and the life of the tree, then the fruit will be trueness of life. It is vain to expect to find any other fruits of the Spirit such as love, or faith, or kindness, or humility, without having truth first of all. There is no love, faith, kindness, or humility that is not an expression of trueness of life.

There are no shortcuts to life. The road has not been widened over the centuries. No accumulation of knowledge or experience or good works can add another lane to the road. The way is the truth and the life, and it is exceedingly narrow. This is the one and only road that God calls men to walk on. Widening the road is simply not an option available to us. What is available is the Spirit of Truth to everyone desirous of walking in the truth. God has no greater joy than this, to see His children walking in the truth.

CHAPTER 6

Absolute Truth
and
the Spirit of the Lie

Coming to a Full Stop

Everyone who has driven a car has had the experience of approaching an intersection, slowing down, glancing both ways, and then choosing either to stop or to slowly slide through. The sign *says* "full stop," but...that is only a guide, a warning; it does not really *mean* "full stop." After all, stopping is so inconvenient, so time-consuming and wasteful of gas and brake linings. It requires going against the momentum of a vehicle already in motion, of a set of well-practiced attitudes and choices in favor of self-assurance, ease and convenience. Therefore, we do not stop. We make truth relative to our own judgment, our own needs, and our own subjectivity. "It says... but it doesn't really mean." Then we wonder why the Spirit seems to be absent from our lives. We are all guilty of this, or offenses like it. We are all, to some degree, in one place or another, not coming to a full stop.

As long as it is convenient and serves our interests, truth, like a stop sign, is obeyed. When there is traffic in the intersection, or we cannot see far enough to proceed safely, we are willing to come to a full stop. But what happens when there seems to be nothing to gain, no apparent benefit from stopping and some obvious benefits to be obtained from coasting through? What happens when we, like Eve in the garden, examine the forbidden fruit before us more closely and determine that it is good for food, beautiful to the eye, and able to make one wise? "God *said* do not eat...but what He really *means* is...It *says* "full stop," but what it really *means* is..." We would never simply disregard a sign. We slow down to provide enough of an appearance of obedience to satisfy ourselves and others, but it is just an appearance. The issue has already been decided. Once truth is made relative to our ends, however base or noble, it has ceased to be an end in itself. Truth that is relative to our ends is our servant. Only truth that is loved and obeyed for its own sake, apart from its apparent utility, is our Lord. Relativism is at the very heart of worldly wisdom. The world celebrates tolerance as a cardinal virtue and is prepared to tolerate everythingæexcept absolute values and absolute truth. To the wisdom and enlightenment of the world, nothing is more offensive than what it calls "dogmatism." However, beneath the world's professed concern for the complexity of circumstances, there lies a rejection of *any* and *all* absolutes. In its zeal against "dogmatism," the world exalts toleration above righteousness, and degrades truth thereby.

Pragmatism vs. Obedience

Relativism has its typical catchphrases: "That may be true for you, but not for me." "It all depends on how you look at it." "Nothing is black and white." Thus adultery, like beauty, is reduced to a function of the eyes of the beholder, and sodomy is reduced to an "alternative lifestyle." All values and judgments dissolve into a pervasive gray haze. That grayness is fatal to truth. It is the result of practicing relativism and mixing right and wrong, white and black, light and dark; but God is light and there is no darkness in Him. Light is truth, and grayness is as much of a deception and a lie as is darkness—if not more. God's first words spoken over a chaotic creation were, "Let there be light," and He separated light from darkness (Gen 1:3-4). That act of separation has never been annulled. Light and darkness cannot mix; neither can truth and falsehood. "Full stop" goes on meaning "full stop," even when it is inconvenient. The world's wisdom is always trying to undo God's eternal, absolute distinctions, always trying to blur the boundary between truth and lies, always seeking to create a gray haze in which to redefine and justify what we desire to be and to do. Relativism is appealing because, unlike truth, it is so convenient!

God's Plumb Line of Truth is Absolute

God has dropped a plumb line down from heaven: absolute truth, absolute righteousness, and absolute love. That plumb line is Jesus Himself. In Him all things hold together. Outside of Him all things fall apart; all things tumble back towards a formless void. The universe does not "approximately" hold together because God is not an approximate God. Jesus is not approximately the truth, the way, and the life. That is why the Redeemer is not very popular. He is absolutely holy and true and terribly inconvenient. When He says "Stop," He does not mean "Slow down and slide through." He comes full of grace...and truth (Jn 1:17). The spirit of this age is wholly antithetical to such a Christ and such a truth. It prefers its truth without teeth, harmless and docile, to be used when convenient and then put quietly back in its place. It prefers the grayness.

One, therefore, expects to find grayness in the world. It was conceived by a lie in the beginning. The serpent said to Eve, "You surely shall not die" (Gen 3:4). This evil age was birthed by the principle that the end justifies the means.

It lives by that principle as its primary creed. The relief of loneliness justifies adultery; the relief of stress and inconvenience justifies abortion; the perfecting of the race justifies genocide. The world is simply fulfilling its spiritual nature when it denies absolute truth. Grayness is its preferred atmosphere, its necessary condition for survival. The Church, however, was begotten by the word of truth. It is the one place on earth where grayness should never be found. God is light and we are children of light. The righteous are characterized by their love for the light (Jn 3:19-21). The light banishes all the varying shades of gray; it makes things manifest. The righteous should have no need to dwell in shadows. They should have no personal ends, no desires that require shadows for their fulfillment and justification. The pallor, the dullness, and the grayness, which are the outward signs of living in a shadow world of partial light, should never be seen among God's people—not in our marriages, not in our worship, and not in our faces—for we are children of light.

Heavenly Truth vs. Worldly Wisdom

The sad truth, however, is that grayness is the mark of far too many Christian lives. The light of truths merely known and professed, but not walked in, is not sufficient to dispel the shadows cast from within by the relativism and pragmatism by which we are living. Our confessions of truth extend only to the boundaries of our own self-interest and convenience. When it comes to the practical issues of our lives and our ministries, we are as relativistic as the world. Our knowledge is heavenly, but our wisdom is the wisdom of the world. We know that the sign says "Stop," but we are all, in some way and in some place, finding a way to justify sliding through.

Every time we do slide through, we pass out of the realm of the Spirit of Truth and enter into the domain and the dominion of the spirit of a lie.

If truth were convenient, then the whole world would be going after it; it is precisely the Spirit of Truth that the world cannot receive. The world does not want the Spirit of Truth because it is an embarrassment, an encumbrance, and a terrible inconvenience. The world has no room for truth; it is too full of its own spirit and wisdom. How many businesses would suffer almost instant collapse and bankruptcy if they resolved to base all of their sales, their advertising and expense accounts on truth and nothing but the truth, in spirit as well as in word? According to the wisdom of the world, a man is a fool if he pays all of his taxes, or returns excess change at the checkout counter, or works a full shift for a full day's pay. That sort of truthfulness is more than foolish in the world—it is dangerous and subversive! It is a threat to the survival of a whole order, a challenge to the premises on which the whole system of the world is based. The world would shake and topple if all of the half-truths, exaggerations, and manipulations that prop it up were suddenly pulled out from under it.

What would happen if churches and Christian ministries resolved to base everything they did on truth alone? Would our mailboxes continue to be filled with some of the appeals that come to us? Would exclamation marks be as prolific? Would everything from "Help!" and "Urgent!" to "Dear Friends" be underlined with a felt-tipped pen? When calculation and manipulation begin to be employed, even in a good cause, the result is deceit. If you yield, even for a moment, to worldly wisdom, and set aside the high standard of conformity to the very Spirit and not just the letter of truth, then you will cross the line of demarcation between the Kingdom and the world.

If you begin by exaggerating your need and justifying your exaggeration because it is, after all, for the sake of "the ministry," then you will end up justifying blatant lies and sins. If you begin by underlining "Urgent" for mere effect, then you will end up underlining "Dear Friends" as well. Once you allow yourself to justify sliding through the stop sign, it is just a matter of time until you disregard the sign altogether.

Truth: A Moment-by-Moment Vigilance

The whole earth is going to be shaken, and that includes the Church. Only that which is unshakable, grounded upon the Rock of Truth, will remain standing. Everything feigned and manipulative, everything corrupted by the self-justifying wisdom of the world, will come crumbling down. In the day of God's judgment, appealing to the end for which we sought will not justify our ungodly means. What is our end if we can even imagine that a corrupt means can be employed to reach it? Truly seeking to glorify and express the truth of God precludes employing manipulation and deceit. We may protest that our ultimate concern is God's glory and God's ministry, but the truth is, if we are employing the wisdom of the world and the spirit of the lie, it is our *own* reputation and our *own* glory that is our end. Truth in the innermost place of our motives requires relentless, daily, moment-by-moment vigilance. Every seemingly small compromise serves to remove us that much further from the Spirit of Truth until the holy dove departs, and we go on, not even realizing that He has left.

The more urgent and the more spiritual the end seems, the more tempting it is to resort to the spirit of the lie to fulfill it. How do you express your need if you are a ministry and unable to house all who are laboring with you as a sub-zero Northern Minnesota winter approaches? How much innuendo, how much implicit suggestion, how many veiled appeals for funds are justified in a newsletter? Even legitimate need will not excuse a lie. If something cannot be spoken in the light, if it requires veiling, suggestion, some sort of shadowy covering, then it should not be spoken at all. There is an alternative to manipulation: trusting God. Speaking truth is evidence of trusting God; it is always an act of faith. The issue of truth is the issue of faith. If we cannot be moved to give, to repent, or to do anything by unadorned truth, then let us not be moved at all. Our love for truth is measured by how far towards perishing we are willing to go without seeking to save ourselves with a lie.

From Jesus' own mouth came a definition of a true Israelite, and by extension we can say, of a true Church. He saw Nathaniel coming towards Him, and He said, **"An Israelite indeed, in whom is no guile!" (Jn 1:47 NAS).** That definition still stands. The Spirit of Christ in us still leaps in recognition when a Nathaniel comes into our presence. Nathaniel had not yet said a word. He had not uttered a single doctrinal truth or factually correct statement at the time that Jesus identified him. He was an Israelite indeed, a true Israelite, recognizable as such not by his words, but by his utter guilelessness. Nathaniel walked in truth, free from all pretense, all hidden meanings, all false appearances. He walked and lived in the light, and it showed.

CHAPTER 7

Truth: A Guileless Spirit

Paul: An Israelite Indeed

Paul was a Nathaniel, an Israelite indeed—and manifestly so, because he was free of guile when it counted.

> **And when I came to you, brethren, I did not come with superiority of speech or of wisdom, proclaiming to you the testimony of God. For I determined to know nothing among you except Jesus Christ, and Him crucified. And I was with you in weakness and in fear and in much trembling. And my message and my preaching were not in persuasive words of wisdom, but in demonstration of the Spirit and of power, that your faith should not rest on the wisdom of men, but on the power of God. (I Cor 2:1-5 NAS).**

No one could doubt that Paul was eloquent. He could speak wisdom, but not the wisdom of this age. His words were spiritual, reserved and fitted for spiritual thoughts. When he was eloquent, his eloquence was transparent; it was completely at the service of truth. It called no attention to itself. The apostle was utterly careless of his reputation. He knew the fine points of Greek oratory; he knew all the ways to win a crowd's admiration with a series of well-turned phrases; he knew the utility of eloquence, good appearance, and adorning his speech with contrived cadences and gestures. However, he was determined not to do so. Paul knew what every lover of truth knows: in order to speak truth, you must demonstrate truth, and in order to demonstrate truth, you must be as humble and transparent as the Spirit of Truth Himself.

Speaking Truth in the Power of the Spirit

Every word Paul spoke was shaped and determined from within by the truth that he was not speaking by his own calculation. Once the nature of truth is recognized, the form and manner of speaking, as much as the content, cease to be at the discretion of the speaker. Paul was determined to know and to communicate nothing but Christ and Him crucified. He was determined not to communicate Paul, not to be concerned for his own glory or reputation. Thus, his very manner of speaking of Christ was itself a crucifixion for Paul. It was a demonstration of a death to all self-serving, all regard for one's own reputation, all desire for effect. This is true not just for Paul. Whenever we speak, we face the same choice that confronted Paul, either to enhance and protect ourselves as speakers or to trust truth to manifest itself. Too often, is not what we do in the name of better communication really done to safeguard against our appearing foolish? We fear embarrassment more than we love truth. Paul spoke not in word only, but in the demonstration and power of the Spirit. Unless we determine to set aside our modern equivalent of Greek oratory and rhetorical flourishes, we will be left with words only, devoid of all demonstration and power.

It is difficult to imagine how foolish Paul appeared in Corinth. The Greeks he spoke to were among the most verbally sophisticated people in the world. They epitomized worldly wisdom. Paul's foolishness in Corinth can only be compared to that of the One who went before him in Israel. When Jesus appeared to Israel, He was like a root out of parched ground. He had no stately form or majesty to appeal to men's eyes.

There was nothing in His appearance to attract men to Himself (Is 53:2-3). Everything that worldly wisdom would dictate to make Jesus more acceptable and appealing, every form of fleshly adornment, was absent. He was the unadorned truth and nothing but the truth. Therefore, He was despised and forsaken, not at all esteemed, but thought a fool and a madman. Men turned their faces from Him. He suffered rejection and ridicule precisely because He was heavenly, unleavened bread. Paul was treated the same way as his Lord, for he was an Israelite indeed, in whom there was no guile.

Confidence in Truth vs. Human Ability

Everything that would make Paul strong, impressive, and secure as a speaker was set aside. He came with fear, weakness, and trembling into the midst of a world filled with its own impressive wisdom. Paul was supremely confident in the power of truth, enough so that he could rely upon it without seeking to assist it by some means of his own. Paul was so set upon God's glory that he was willing to face ridicule and rejection, rather than detract from the demonstration of the power of truth. His weakness and trembling are the inevitable condition of every minister standing before a congregation, of every evangelist, of every Christian walking out a day of his life in the midst of the world—every one, that is, who shares Paul's love of truth and his jealousy over God's glory. Paul endured what he did so that our faith might be in God, so that we might be moved and persuaded by the truth and not by some skillful marketing technique born of the pride and insecurity of the speaker, who could not and would not love and trust the truth.

The issue that Paul faced in speaking in Corinth is exactly the same issue we face every morning before the mirror: Am

I free from all guile? Then why do I style myself the way that I do? Paul spoke only those words that were transparent and that let the light of truth pass through from within, without reflecting any light back upon himself. Paul spoke the truth, and only the truth, at all times. What do the clothes, the jewelry, the hairstyles, and the perfumes that I wear speak? Do they magnify God or myself?

Peter addressed women specifically, but his words apply to the Church as the bride of Christ:

> **Let not yours be the outward adorning with braiding of hair, decoration of gold, and wearing of fine clothes, but let it be the hidden person of the heart with the imperishable jewel of a gentle and quiet spirit, which in God's sight is very precious. (I Pe 3:3-4 RSV).**

Likewise Paul wrote,

> **I want women to adorn themselves with proper clothing, modestly and discreetly, not with braided hair and gold or pearls or costly garments; but rather by means of good works, as befits women making a claim to godliness.**
> **(I Tim 2:9-10 NAS).**

Peter and Paul were no more advocating shabbiness and rags in these passages than Paul was advocating bad grammar and poor logic to the Corinthians. The issue is one of motives and of faith. Do I hesitate before the mirror, or before the pulpit, lest I detract from the glory of the Spirit of Truth?

The End Dictates the Means

Am I content to let what I am show through? Am I so devoted to truth, so intent on expressing truth in all things that I will not allow my manner of speech, or the clothes I wear, or the way I present myself to create an impression, an image that is not true? The temptation to alter my image, to add a bit of illusion to the truth, is very powerful. The temptation to justify my self-enhancement as a way of better and more impressively serving God is equally great, but a lie can never serve the God of truth. Every false image is a lie. Everything done from a motive of vanity, pride, and insecurity is a lie. Am I trusting God to live and do and be through me, or am I continually fabricating some kind of image, physical or spiritual, some character that is external only and offering that to God to use and do with and speak through? The end never justifies the means; the end dictates the means. If the end is the revelation of a God who is the truth, then the means must be truth in every aspect of my life.

You *Can* Tell a Book by its Cover

The world is so acclimated to false appearances that it holds as an uncontested principle of wisdom that you can't tell a book by its cover. However, you could tell Nathaniel by his cover; and you could see the Father in His Son. When the Spirit of Truth is fully present, reigning within, He will express Himself outwardly through everything, from the words of a sermon to the hairstyle of the preacher. The fact is, you can always tell a book by its cover. Nothing about a life is merely superficial. Everything, from the surface down, expresses what is the deepest within. If what is deepest is vanity or fear for one's reputation, then that will be what shows itself outwardly. Try as we may to keep our secret heart hidden, it remains true that everything hidden will be revealed.

> **My teaching is not my own," Jesus said. "It comes from Him who sent me...He who speaks on his own does so to gain honor for himself, but he who works for the honor of the one who sent him is a man of truth; there is nothing false about him. (Jn 7:16,18 NIV).**

I can speak true words, but if I make them my own, that is, if I employ them for a self-serving end, then I am not a man of truth. Jesus allowed for only one motive to the man who speaks on his own: to gain honor for himself. Whether from vanity or insecurity, to seek one's own honor is to cease to be true. Then what about my praying, my manner of dress, or my facial expressions? Is my objective to gain recognition, power, or honor for myself? Is there yet something that lingers in my soul that makes me relish and delight in my ability to impress, to manipulate, to control others, with my body, my makeup, my words—my prayers? If we love truth, then these are the type of questions we will be asking ourselves. It simply is not enough to have Jesus say of me, "He spoke no false words." His pleasure and approval are conveyed only when He can say of someone, "He is a man of truth, and there is nothing false about him."

The Subtleties of Deceit

There is an unspoken covenant between the deceiver and the deceived that allows the pretense to go on. There is no preacher who allows himself to become a performer without a congregation willing to become an audience. There is a self-serving end for both. The flatterer and the flattered, the seducer and the seduced, have both ceased to love truth for the same self-gratifying reasons.

Our spirits should wince every time an assembly of God's people are referred to as an "audience". In truth, that is precisely all too often what it is: an audience, enjoying—as well as prompting—the performance of the man on the stage. He who preaches plays his part well and receives his reward from those who came to see and hear him. He knows how to stir the emotions. His voice rises and falls evocatively as he prays; his bearing and manner fulfill our image of what we expect and desire a preacher to be. The words are correct, even stirring, but the spirit of the speaker is saying, "It's all right; I don't really expect you to be changed by this. I'm just doing my part in an unspoken agreement, and you are doing yours, but we know that it is really all just a show."

We have become the willing accomplices in each other's lies. No one is willing to call the other's bluff for fear of having his own bluff called. Truth has become just as relative and captive to our own needs and wants as it is for unbelievers. And as long as truth is suppressed in us, we will be kept from being Nathaniels to a world beguiled and bewitched by the subtleties of deceit.

We have been accomplices in each other's illusions. We need, and are called to be, accomplices in each other's sanctification. We need one another desperately. There is no one without a blind spot. We are all apt to be hypocrites. If we cannot and will not confront one another in love, then we will go on being the prisoners of our own illusions. We are afraid to hurt and to offend, so we remain silent and call our silence love. What we desperately need, and what true love instills, is a greater sense of horror at the sight of lies eating away the souls of those around us. Love constrains us to speak, not to remain silent; for if zeal for God's house and the purity of His word does not consume us, then the spirit of the lie will.

The Spirit of Truth Allows No Compromise

Paul was unafraid to appear weak and foolish to the Corinthians. He was equally unafraid to appear bold and to risk offending men, even to risk offending the apostle Peter at Antioch. To the Galatians he wrote of the time in Jerusalem when false brothers pressed him on the issue of circumcision. **"We did not yield in subjection to them for even an hour, so that the truth of the gospel might remain with you." (Gal 2:5 NAS).** He would not yield even for a moment, because to do so would allow leaven to enter into the lump. It would have been convenient to let Peter's subsequent hypocrisy in Antioch pass. Why risk offending a pillar of the Church, especially when you are not one of the original twelve yourself? Why risk appearing as an upstart? Why risk being rebuffed by Peter in the presence of those whom you have won to Christ? No one wants to be labeled as fanatical, legalistic, or unloving. However, because Paul was himself a man of the truth, he knew by the Spirit of Truth in him when an issue allowed for no compromise. He knew the difference between discretion and cowardice, between self-righteousness and a zeal for the integrity of God's truth. He knew when love compelled him to confront the hypocrisy of a brother.

Gentleness and Boldness: One Source

Paul was a latecomer to the gospel, he had been a persecutor of the Church, and in Antioch he found himself face-to-face with Peter, who was one of the three that had been closest to Jesus. The same Paul who stood before the Corinthians in fear and great trembling now stood before Peter and opposed him to his face (Gal 2:11-14). What moved Paul to appear weak and foolish at one time was precisely the same thing that moved him to be bold and confront Peter at another. His weakness and his boldness, his gentleness and his firmness, had one source, one purpose animating them: a passionate devotion to the purity and truth of the gospel.

Paul had observed Peter willingly eating together with Gentile believers, until a band of Jewish believers, who still kept the old ordinance against eating with Gentiles, arrived. At that point, Peter's behavior changed.

> **For prior to the coming of certain men from James, he used to eat with the Gentiles; but when they came, he began to withdraw and hold himself aloof, fearing the party of the circumcision. (Gal 2:12 NAS).**

Peter's change was not born out of deference or love, but out of his fear of men. Paul watched while someone as broken and gifted as Peter succumbed to fear of disapproval and rejection, descending into hypocrisy. Every lie has at its root some self-serving purpose. Abraham told Sarah to lie and say that she was his sister, "that it may be well with me" (Gen 12:13). There is no freedom from the temptation and the power of lies so long as there is a "me" seeking to be pampered and protected.

Only a Crucified Life ...

If even Peter was not immune to such temptation, then we would be very foolish to imagine that we are. If Peter needed a Paul to confront him, then we would be very foolish to think that we can keep ourselves true alone. But who will confront me in my hypocrisy if he is ensnared in hypocrisy himself? Had Paul been ruled by fear of men, had he still been addicted to and dependent upon men's approval and praise, he could never have confronted Peter. The fear of man, the fear of rejection, the fear of ridicule, has a way of turning the strongest knees to jelly. Only a man like Paul, whose only boast was in the cross of Christ, who was a dead man brought back to life in Christ, could rise above fear and speak to Peter in truth and love. Only a crucified life, and not merely the doctrine of the cross, will set us free from fear of men and enable us to confront, when necessary, the Peters of our own generation.

> **And the rest of the Jews joined him in hypocrisy, with the result that even Barnabas was carried away by their hypocrisy. But when I saw that they were not straightforward [lit. walking straightly] about the truth of the gospel, I said to Cephas** *in the presence of them all.*
> **(Gal 2:13-14 NAS)** [brackets and emphasis added]

A little leaven leavens the whole lump. Peter's hypocrisy was contagious. It quickly spread, probably without a word having to be spoken. Action really does speak louder than words. The price of tolerating a lie does not remain constant; it increases and continues to increase until it is paid in full. Present pain avoided becomes a greater pain later. Truth is not convenient, and as long as we prefer and choose comfort and convenience, we will not walk in the truth. The spirit of the lie will provide convenience and self-gratification and self-justification for everyone who seeks them. It will seek to convince us that it is not necessary to suffer in any way, that pain can and should be avoided. That which is true and unfeigned is always costly. It requires putting away that which is false. The way of truth is always the way of the cross. It is a death to confront a brother in love and a death to allow one's self to be confronted.

Walking in Truth: The Choice of the Cross

We have worn crosses around our necks and attached them to the dashboards of our cars, but a dedication to truth will inevitably transform the cross from harmless decoration into a very real, daily experience. Purging the spirit of the lie is not painless. Every compromise, every exaggeration, and every lie is, in essence, an avoidance of humiliation and death. Like the serpent's first lie in the garden, every lie since is calculated to appeal to and exalt ambition, vanity, self-gratification, and pride; that is, everything that crucified the Lord, and everything He died to set us free from. The choice to walk in the truth is the choice to take up one's cross and follow Him daily. That is why truth is not very popular, why it is far easier to talk about it than to walk in it. Turning a pragmatic truce in a marriage into a real peace will require a measure of anguish and travail. This is why pragmatic truces tend to become as much the norm in Christian marriages as in worldly ones.

To slow down and barely slide through a stop sign is not ninety percent obedience; it is one hundred percent failure to stop. To exaggerate just a little, to perform and manipulate emotions from behind the pulpit just a little, to pretend and to posture just a little is to lie completely. We seem to have brought our experience of the classroom over into our relationship with God. We come to the Lord as students to their teacher at the start of the school year, asking, "What is the minimum I have to do to 'get by'?" What is the passing grade for this Christian life? Will sixty-five percent truth do? Truth is absolute, and something is either the whole truth, or it is not truth at all. Such absoluteness is very foreign to us. We have been so thoroughly schooled in the relativism of the world that it seems incredible that God's passing grade could actually be one hundred percent. Even the least bit of leaven still leavens the whole lump.

The choice between truth and a lie, between integrity and convenience, is put before us repeatedly, daily. It is as frequent and as significant as a stop sign. Until we resolve to come to a full stop, to become absolute about truth and integrity, instead of seeking the minimum amount whereby we can 'get by,' our lives will remain devoid of real power, perhaps full of much sound and fury, but where it counts, signifying nothing. Ironically, by seeking the minimum of truth, we condemn ourselves to experiencing a minimal grace and forgiveness. God does not offer just enough grace to get by. His forgiveness when we fall short is as absolute as the goal He sets. He who aims for less than the whole truth will find himself experiencing less than the whole of forgiveness. Freedom from condemnation and despair comes from aiming higher, not lower.

"The kingdom of God consists of and is based on not talk but power—moral power and excellence of soul." (I Cor 4:20 Amplified). Moral power and excellence of soul are not attained by sliding through stop signs, regardless of how much we slow down. They are rather the fruit and the evidence of having come to a full stop. There is a task before us. There is a full stop that needs making in our work places and bedrooms, behind our pulpits and in our casual conversations, before our mirrors and in our prayers. God waits for His children to embrace and walk in truth—absolutely. His Spirit is poured out without measure upon those who are whole-hearted in their devotion to truth. We need to pray earnestly together for the grace to break the power of the spirit of the lie and to walk in truth before God and the world.

Lord, if ever we have asked that we be not hearers of the word only, but doers, we ask it now; even as we ask, we tremble, for we acknowledge that we do not have the courage for this. We are cowards, we are afraid of what men will say, we are afraid of what our husbands or our wives will say or do. We don't know how to relate to each other. We do not even know how to begin to speak the things that are true; we have been silent for too long. We have been satisfied too long with just "getting by." What You have called us to is a revolution, and we do not have any stomach for that, because we have to admit that we prefer convenience to truth. But, precious God, we love You, and we desire to see Your Kingdom established in the earth. How can we call You the King of kings and not yield to the Kingdom way? So, Lord, we just ask You for grace and mercy as we seek to walk in truth. We want You to rejoice. We want to see Your heart gladdened, and we are sick and tired of just merely mouthing "hallelurah" and "amens" and singing choruses. We want You really to have satisfaction and joy as you look upon Your children who walk in the truth. So, Lord, help us. Let it begin today. Show us in Your gentle way, by the Spirit, where we need to make corrections, where we have been slipping through the full stop signs and have not noticed. Show us that when You say "full stop," You mean full stop. When You say "love," You mean love; when You say "truth," You mean truth...not "approximately" or "kind of" but actually, perfectly, totally. I ask Your blessing, Lord, on us, that to the degree that our hearts are determined to walk in this way, Your grace shall lead us where the tire meets the road. May we dare to live by faith, willing also to perish if You be not the God who brings life out of death. We would rather fail than "get by." May we enter a realm of Your grace that we have never before known and may the grayness be dispelled from our lives, from our marriages, and from our congregations, as an increasing measure of light and joy come with the coming of Your reality and truth. Thank You for being a God of urgent speaking, for being a God of truth. We love You and praise You for being such a One. In Jesus' name, we pray. Amen.

CHAPTER 8

Humility: The Way of Truth

Redefining the Part as the Whole

There is an incident recorded in the fifth chapter of the Book of Acts concerning the sale of a piece of real estate. Had this episode taken place in our present generation, it would have had an entirely different conclusion. If some contemporary Ananias and Sapphira brought the proceeds, no doubt considerable, from the sale of their property to the elders of their church, they would likely be celebrated and applauded. The esteem in which their spirituality was regarded would increase greatly. Ananias might be assured a place on the church board or a position as an elder or a deacon. But this incident occurred in another age, in an hour when the Spirit of God prevailed in such magnitude and purity. That same act, which might well be celebrated today, resulted in sudden judgment and death. We can only suspect that the Church has moved a long distance away from the purity, power, and relentless pursuit of truth that characterized it at its inception. Thankfully, there is a God who has not changed and who is intent upon returning us to that same high standard.

> **But a certain man named Ananias, with his wife Sapphira, sold a piece of property, and kept back some of the price for himself, with his wife's full knowledge, and bringing a portion of it, he laid it at the apostles' feet. But Peter said, "Ananias, why has Satan filled your heart to lie to the Holy Spirit, and to keep back some of the**

price of the land? While it remained unsold, did it not remain your own? And after it was sold, was it not under your control? Why is it that you have conceived this deed in your heart? You have not lied to men, but to God." And as he heard these words, Ananias fell down and breathed his last; and great fear came upon all who heard of it. (Ac 5:1-5 NAS).

Ananias and Sapphira probably brought an impressive sum. Their sin was not that they were stingy, but that they made what they gave appear to be a whole when it was only a part, however great that part may have been. We might be tempted to ask ourselves, "Was what they did really so wrong? After all, if I give a large sum, isn't that virtually the same as giving all that I have? The fact is, I am keeping back only a small portion for myself, so it isn't really a lie to say I gave all. It really is as if I had laid the whole amount that I had in the offering basket. If some people in the church conclude from my generosity that I gave all that I had, it would be "legalistic" and "literalistic" to correct them. Anyway, compared to what others in the church are giving, my portion really is the equivalent of giving all. It represents a total amount." So the logic behind Ananias and Sapphira's act goes. They were not the last Christians to redefine the part as the whole and to justify letting it appear as such! Peter did not operate according to that sort of logic. He discerned by the Spirit of Truth, and he unmasked and confronted Ananias and Sapphira's lie. They may have succeeded in deceiving themselves, but not the Holy Spirit. Ananias and Sapphira were not only liars, but also thieves. Every liar is a thief, because every lie is a way of obtaining what is not rightfully his.

Abundant Grace and Wholeheartedness

The verses immediately before the story of Ananias and Sapphira describe a church in which,

> **Those who believed were of one heart and soul; and not one of them claimed that anything belonging to him was his own; but all things were common property to them...there was not a needy person among them, for all who were owners of lands or houses would sell them and bring the proceeds of the sales, and lay them at the apostles' feet.**
> **(Ac 4:32-35 NAS).**

The Church in Jerusalem was wholehearted, and one result was that **"with great power the apostles were giving witness to the resurrection of the Lord Jesus, and abundant grace was upon them all." (Ac 4:33 NAS).** Ananias and Sapphira lived in the midst of that Church. They saw the abundant grace, the joy, and the depth of communion that was being experienced by people who had given all. They desired that abundant grace for themselves, but they failed to make the connection between such grace and the wholeheartedness of those who were experiencing it. They had seen Barnabas and others come and lay their gifts at the apostles' feet. They did the same, but only in appearance, only outwardly. They sought to obtain power, joy, and great grace by bringing only a part, in place of the whole.

We need to ask ourselves, are we doing anything different from what Ananias and Sapphira did when we seek and expect abundant grace and power, while giving ourselves only in part, while claiming to have given ourselves wholly? We all want the abundant grace, the profound comfort, the intimate communion that acknowledging and walking in all of truth imparts, but we want it at the price of acknowledging truth only as words and doctrines. We want to speak truths but not to be true, to possess truth but not to obey it. We are bringing our partial, verbal truth and laying it at the feet of the apostolic standard and wanting our portion to be accepted as the whole! After all, isn't our orthodox, evangelical, fundamental, pentecostal affirmation really so much greater than that of so many other Christians? We may have retained a small portion for ourselves, that is, the right to exaggerate now and again, to speak a few "white" lies, to appear to be what we are not. No one is perfect, and to insist upon walking in truth is to be legalistic, after all. Therefore, the rationalizations continue with us just as with Ananias and Sapphira. The reality is that if we claim to be men and women of truth, while inwardly reserving the right to be untrue, justifying little compromises and hypocrisies, then we have presented the part as the whole and purposed in our hearts to lie to the Holy Spirit. James wrote that the violation of one commandment was the breaking of the whole law (Jas 2:10). Deciding to tolerate one deceit is to violate the whole truth. To be ninety-nine percent true and represent it as the whole truth is to lie utterly.

Truth that is not the whole truth is not the truth *at all*. The man who embraces most of the truth is not necessarily any closer to the truth than the one who affirms none of it. In fact, he may be much further from it. It is remarkable how far some people are prepared to go in acknowledging who Jesus is. They think themselves quite generous when they recognize Him as a great prophet and teacher and moral example. We tend to applaud such "openness." We are quick to become excited about how close to salvation such a person seems to be. After all, they have assented to ninety percent of the truth. How could someone have such insight, how could they grasp so many spiritual truths, and still be enemies of truth? How many Christians have felt intimidated and foolish in the presence of such a "truth-seeker," unable to insist upon that last missing portion? "Surely such a person is, in effect, as much a Christian as I am. Surely his part, being so great, being so close to the whole, really is equivalent to the whole." If we have not understood the nature of truth, we will be just so intimidated. If we do not insist upon the whole truth for ourselves, then we will falter and step back from insisting upon it for another.

Embracing the Whole Truth

To acknowledge Jesus as prophet and teacher, yet to refuse to affirm *all* that He said about Himself is to deny Him completely. Such partial acknowledgment is not to be applauded; it is cause for the greater concern because it is a partial truth offered in place of the whole. Therefore, it is a perilous deceit and a lie. Someone may be prepared to bring a very generous portion of the praise and acclaim due to Jesus and not the whole, but it is the part retained that makes all the difference.

It is that final portion of truth that decides our relationship to truth. The scripture that offends our pride, that goes against the grain of our own understanding, that is likely to offend others, is the one that matters most. That last statement, which, if finally affirmed, really gives God final authority in our lives, determines everything. Yes, I believe all that Scripture teaches, except...about hell...about judgment... about authority. Yes, I believe God is just and sovereign in all His deeds, except in this tragedy, except in this personal loss. I'll give thanks and praise to Him in all circumstances, except for this one. The issue of belief, of love, of lordship, depends not upon the belief or love or submission we find it easy to give, but upon the part we are most tempted to keep back for ourselves.

Peter said to Ananias, **"You have not lied to men, but to God." (Ac 5:4 NAS).** To whom do we think we are lying when we give ourselves in part and represent it as the whole, when we worship in part, pray in part, love in part, believe in part? **"And as he heard *these words,* Ananias fell down and breathed his last; and great fear came upon all who heard of it." (Ac 5:5 NAS).** It was when Ananias heard "these words" that the full magnitude of his deception broke upon him. "You have not lied only to men; you have not deceived only yourself. Your rationalizations, your self-justifications, your boasting in being a lover of truth, while refusing to assent to all that God has spoken, constitute a lie to God Himself." Does the judgment that came upon Ananias and Sapphira seem far too harsh, too severe to us? Until we perceive the magnitude of their sin, as well as our own, their judgment will remain an offense and a mystery to us. Ananias and Sapphira never denied that Christ came in the flesh. They never denied His bodily resurrection. They never contradicted a single doctrine of the faith. Yet, for their deceit they received an instant judgment. That judgment was a statement of how much value God places upon truth. That high value was communicated to the whole Church. **"Great fear came upon the whole church and upon all who heard of these things." (Ac 5:11 NAS).** They were all braced and sobered by the fear that they, too, might be carried out and buried, not for just a breach of orthodoxy, but for presenting to God a part and calling it the whole.

The Fear of the God of Truth

How many of us would like to see the Spirit of God acting as severely with those of us who have indulged in deception and half-truths in our own generation as the Spirit did in theirs? There is an absence in our generation of the "great fear" that came upon the Church in Jerusalem, an absence of the awe and trembling that filled believers who stood before a God who would not countenance a lie. It is no coincidence that this high regard for truth and this holy fear of the God of truth are not the only things missing from our generation. The very next verse begins,

> **Now by the hands of the apostles...numerous and startling signs and wonders were being performed among the people...there were being added to the Lord those who believed...so that they [even] kept carrying out the sick into the streets and placing them on couches and sleeping pads [in the hope] that as Peter passed by at least his shadow might fall on some of them. And the people gathered also from the towns and hamlets around Jerusalem, bringing the sick and those troubled with foul spirits, and they were all cured. (Ac 5:12-16 Amplified).**

The Spirit of God was present in great power to heal the sick and to bring many to repentance in the very same hour that Peter was moved by the same Spirit to confront Ananias and Sapphira. That power is absent today, and it will not be restored to the Church until the Church is restored to the standard of truth that God established in the beginning.

That men and women are not being struck dead instantly in our congregations is not a statement of God's tolerance of our deceits and lies. Judgment may not be as sudden, but it is no less certain. **"Bread obtained by falsehood is sweet to a man, but afterwards his mouth will be filled with gravel." (Pr 20:17 NAS).** How much of the esteem, the joy, the prestige, and the peace presently being enjoyed in the Church is destined to turn to gravel in our mouths? It tastes sweet at the moment. There has been no Peter to challenge us. Truth has fallen into low regard, and there is little, if any, fear of the God who hates lies in any form. "White lies" and exaggerations and subtle misrepresentations are so frequent as to be considered normal, if not even desirable and required, in the conduct of Christian life. The perverse logic of deceit is made to seem true after all. If the ministers of God who transgress against truth are not being struck down like Ananias and Sapphira, God must have changed, or else truth has changed since the days of the Book of Acts. The reality is that God has not changed. Our lies are still killing us, only more slowly. We are starving, because the bread of deceit, no matter how sweet and plentiful, is not real food.

Every lie is an act of astonishing presumption. What must take place within my heart for me to believe that God does not discern my deceit? I must exalt my own rationalizations above the Spirit of God. Every lie is an elevation of self above truth, above the one lied to. I cannot lie to someone and still regard him as greater or even equal. The very act of lying lifts me above the one deceived; it lowers him in my sight. By lying to the Holy Spirit, Ananias and Sapphira were exalting themselves above God.

It is not surprising, then, that Peter said to Ananias, **"Why has Satan filled your heart to lie to the Holy Spirit?" (Ac 5:3).** The devil was a liar from the beginning, and he is the father of lies (Jn 8:44). He is also the father of pride. His fall was an act of self-exaltation, a supreme presumption to ascend up to the level of God Himself. His pride is itself a lie, an assertion of being more than He in whom truth resides. Pride and deceit have been intimately related from the beginning. They have a common nature, a common source. It was indeed nothing less than Satan that filled Ananias' heart, just as surely as it was no one less than God to whom Ananias lied.

Every Lie has Root in the Father of Lies

Ananias' lie implied the presence and working of the spirit of the lie in his heart. Every lie has its root and inspiration in the father of lies, but the operation of that spirit in no way exonerated Ananias. In the very next verse Peter asks Ananias, **"Why is it that you have conceived this deed in your heart?" (Ac 5:4).** Satan filled, and Ananias conceived. Ananias was no innocent victim; he was a full and intimate accomplice. He welcomed the deceit and willingly agreed with it. Ananias and Sapphira were no more innocent than were Adam and Eve in the garden when the serpent came and offered them the first lie: "You shall not die." They proceeded to reach up and eat the fruit that promised exaltation and equality with God. Every lie is an assertion of self, a lifting of self above truth to a level equal to the Author of truth—God Himself. It is a satanic defiance of God. Pride and presumption invite and draw to themselves the father of lies. The ground is well fertilized with rationalizations and justifications. Once a heart is filled with such arguments, it is only a matter of time before every sort of lie is conceived. Satan comes to such a heart, and he finds much opportunity in it.

The Character of the King

When the devil came to Jesus, he found nothing in Him. Jesus was utterly true. There was nothing in Him that could receive and nurture a lie. There was no desire to exceed the bounds of truth. That yielding to the limits God has given us is true humility, and it is the essence of walking in truth. Jesus is the truth because He is perfectly and truly humble.

Do nothing from selfishness or empty conceit, but with humility of mind let each of you regard one another as more important than himself... Have this attitude in yourselves which was also in Christ Jesus, who, although He existed in the form of God, did not regard equality with God a thing to be grasped, but emptied Himself, taking the form of a bondservant, and being made in the likeness of men. (Phil 2:3-7 NAS).

These verses describe the mystery of the incarnation of God in human flesh. They are applicable to all of us who are called sons of God. As such, we are afforded every opportunity and temptation to exalt ourselves and become arrogant. It is tempting to derive from our sonship an elevated, grand image of ourselves; therefore, we need all the more to be reminded of the character of the King and His Kingdom. Jesus came down from above and never once lifted Himself up again. **"And being found in appearance as a man, He humbled Himself by becoming obedient to the point of death, even death on a cross." (Phil 2:8 NAS).** His humility was not in part. It did not stop short of totality. He refused, without reservation or limit, to defend Himself, to save some last shred of reputation and image, to spare Himself the supreme pain of rejection and misunderstanding. He was utterly true and humble. No appeal to save and exalt Himself, to the amount of "good" He could do for God, could take root in His heart. Not even the sight of pained confusion and disappointment in the faces of His followers could provoke Him to save Himself. The disgrace and humiliation of the cross was the final test, the perfection of His humility and the sealing of His character. Paul writes, **"Have this attitude in yourselves which was also in Christ Jesus." (Phil 2:5).**

How are we, as well as the world, going to recognize a people who live in all of the truth of the gospel? How will people know that we are indeed children of the King? It is neither going to be by seeing how highly we exalt ourselves, nor by the grandiose architecture of our meeting places, nor by the size and wealth of our ministries. The sure sign that we are in the truth, and in the One who is true, is that we have this attitude in us that was in Him. It is vain to boast about having the "full gospel" when you have only the smallest part of the character of the One that gospel is about.

Humility: Our Need—God's Provision

"Do nothing from selfishness or empty conceit." (Phil 2:3). The elimination of such motives from the heart would render one instantly true, because lying and deceit would have no ground left in which to be conceived. But how do I go about obeying such an exhortation when the temptations toward selfishness and empty conceit are so powerful and subtle and ever-present? No wonder Paul goes on to say, **"Work out your salvation with fear and trembling." (Phil 2:12). The Amplified Bible says, "Work out, cultivate, carry out to the goal and fully complete, your own salvation with reverence and awe and trembling [self-distrust, that is, with serious caution, tenderness of conscience,**

watchfulness against temptation].'' (Phil 2:12 Amplified).
The requirement to be true is itself overwhelming, once it is
fully grasped. The requirement to be humble and to have this
mind in us that was also in Christ as the ground and basis for
being true is even more exacting. There is a fearful diligence
that characterizes the one who has glimpsed the subtlety and
pervasiveness of his own selfishness and pride and who has
sensed the real meaning and value of truth. That fearfulness
and trembling heightens one's sensitivity to the presence of
the stop signs of the Spirit. It heightens one's awareness of
what every gesture and intonation of voice and expression of
face is communicating.

**"Work out your salvation with fear and trembling, for
it is God who is at work in you, both to will and to work
for His good pleasure." (Phil 2:12-13 NAS).** Knowing that
it is God in us, willing and doing what pleases Himself, should
cause us all the more to tremble, but the trembling that this
knowledge produces is not the sort that paralyzes and drives
one to despair. This ultimate source of trembling is at the
same time the ultimate source of hope. As the Spirit of Truth
is provided to fulfill the requirement to be true, so the Spirit of
Christ—God in us—is the provision to fulfill the requirement
to be humble. God's provision is hidden to the man who still
believes in his heart that he has no need of it. The one who still
believes that he can be like Christ, even in Christ's humility,
the one for whom the mind of Christ, like trueness of life, is
still his own accomplishment and good work, is left blind to
God's provision. The belief that I can attain humility is the
ultimate conceit. The imitation, the simulation in my own
strength of the mind that was in Christ Jesus is the ultimate
act of hubris and the most vain and blasphemous of lies. It
is an exaltation of self and a misconception of humility. It is

the failure to see humility as a state of being to which only the Spirit of God can bring one.

Who is Sufficient?

The provision of God is reserved for the man who cries out with Paul, **"Who is sufficient for these things?" (II Cor 2:16).** The realization that it is God in us who is willing and doing, while producing fear and trembling at the same time, produces the ultimate humility that sets us free to become true. The truth is, we cannot do it ourselves. It takes God in us to make us like Jesus, to make us true. The final salvation from the tyranny of self comes with the revelation that we cannot make ourselves humble or true. We have only to wholeheartedly desire and intend it. We cannot perfect ourselves, and what is more humbling or true than that?

We want to arise, to ascend, to go up, but we seem almost incapable of apprehending that God's path to the high place to which we aspire is one that always leads down. The realization of God in us making us true is a humbling, a lowering of our souls. Jesus came down from heaven to earth, down from divinity to washing the feet of His own disciples, down to the Jordan, down into baptism, down into disrepute, rejection, weakness and into a naked, humiliating death. **"Therefore God also highly exalted Him, and bestowed on Him the name which is above every name." (Phil 2:9 NAS).** Every lie is a self-exaltation. Pride is capable only of reaching up. If we are to become true, then we are going to have to descend, not rise, into all the truth.

What Goes Up Must *First* Go Down

Now this expression, 'He ascended,' what does it mean except that He also had descended into the lower parts of the earth? He who descended is Himself also He who ascended far above all the heavens, that He might fill all things. (Eph 4:9-10 NAS).

In the divine economy, that which goes up must first go down. Anyone who enters into the truths of God in any other way is a thief. You cannot climb over the wall. You cannot use intellect or emotion or spiritual experience to vault over it in order to obtain divine truth. Attempting to do so is itself irrefutable proof that one is an acquirer, as opposed to being a lover, of truth. The lover is the one who is drawn towards and enters through the gate of humility; he is the one who hears his Master's voice and follows Him. The Spirit of Christ leads him into all truth along a path of ever-increasing humility. Within the bounds of truth, lawfully entered, there are sufficient insights and experiences to satisfy the keenest intellect and the most sensitive soul. They are rendered benign and pure only by humility. Having this mind in us, which was in Him, is the beginning and the end of becoming true.

Jesus' Triumphal Entry

Jesus made yet another descent that is recorded in Scripture, which has come to be known as His triumphal entry into Jerusalem. The word "triumphal" suggests a mile long cavalcade of cars with polished chrome gleaming, motorcycle escorts, banners streaming, and all of the accouterments of pomp and grandeur. However, Jesus' entry into Jerusalem was riding on the back of the foal of a donkey, down from the

Mount of Olives. The colt was so young that no one had ever sat upon it. The scene is a picture of absurdity: a loping figure, jerking and halting, a young colt with a grown man upon its back, Jesus' legs almost touching the ground. *This* was the coming of the King into Jerusalem. No gold and splendor, no trumpets, no sedan chair carried by servants. **"This took place," Matthew comments, "to fulfill what was spoken by the prophet, saying, 'Tell the daughter of Zion, 'Behold, your King is coming to you, humble, and mounted on an ass, and on a colt, the foal of an ass.'"** (Mt 21:4-5 RSV).

The initial response of the people was to rejoice greatly even as Zechariah the prophet had said (Zec 9:9):

> **And those who went before and those who followed cried out, 'Hosannah! Blessed is He who comes in the name of the Lord! Blessed is the kingdom of our father David that is coming!' (Mk 11:9-10 RSV).**

Their response proved short-lived, though. Just a short time later, Jesus stood lamenting over a Jerusalem that was rejecting Him and His Kingdom, refusing the comfort of God and leaving no expectation before itself but that of devastation and judgment:

> **Oh Jerusalem, Jerusalem, killing the prophets and stoning those who are sent to you!...Behold, your house is forsaken and desolate. For I tell you, you will not see me again, until you say, 'Blessed is he who comes in the name of the Lord.' (Mt 23:37-39 RSV).**

Desiring His Humility More Than His Power

Our response to God and His Spirit has not changed much since then. The power and exhilaration of the Spirit is what we first notice and respond to. We are quick to shout "Hosannah!" but very slow to recognize the implications of the humble foal that the Lord seeks out and upon which He chooses to come. Only belatedly do we begin to realize that the donkey's colt is no accident, no dispensable detail, but an inseparable part of the coming of the King. He cannot come into His Church or the world except in and by the most perfect humility. It is His nature, His very name. One can almost hear the Spirit, looking down upon the Jerusalem of this present generation, repeating Jesus' words, "You will not see Me again, not in the power and authority and reality that was in the beginning, until you can say, `Blessed is he who comes, not in pomp but in lowliness, not in arrogance and prestige but in humility on the back of a donkey's foal, in the name of the Lord.'" If we are going to receive the Spirit of the Lord in power, without measure, then we are going to have to welcome Him and desire Him and esteem Him as lowly—and to desire His humility for ourselves more than His power. If He is not welcome in humility, then we will face the prospect of having our house left forsaken and desolate.

How is the Spirit of Christ going to come into a world desperate for reality and truth? He needs a body to indwell; He needs flesh and blood to convey the very Spirit of Jesus. We have been busy preparing ourselves with all the riches of the world. We have supposed that what He is waiting for is a Church confident of its power, able to match and outdo the world in assertiveness, grandeur, and wealth, when He has actually been waiting for a very different Church, a very different Body in which to convey Himself to the world—a

Church that most resembles a lowly donkey, a colt, the foal of an ass. We—and the world—shall not see Him again until we are willing to be that.

If at the heart of a lie is pride and arrogance, then at the heart of the truth is humility. Dishonesty is inseparable from pride; it can inhabit and express itself only through self-assertiveness, self-serving, and self-glorification. The spirit of a lie seeks out a body commensurate with its nature. It is at home with arrogance and presumption. The Spirit of Truth cannot and will not indwell and bless such a body. The disciples received the Spirit in full measure because they were brought down into humility and truth. That pattern has not been and will not be changed. All good things come down from heaven to those lowly enough to receive them. If we are waiting patiently, faithfully serving our Master in the daily, mundane requirements of life, tethered like that donkey, beside the Calvary road, Jesus will know where we are. He will call for us at the right time, and we will enter His Kingdom with Him.

The New Jerusalem

There is yet one more instance in Scripture of something coming down from above:

> **And I saw the holy city, new Jerusalem, coming down out of heaven from God, made ready as a bride adorned for her husband...and one of the seven angels...came and spoke with me, saying, 'Come here, I shall show you the bride, the wife of the lamb.' And he carried me away in the Spirit to a great and high mountain, and showed me the holy city, Jerusalem, coming down out**

> of heaven from God, having the glory of God.
> Her brilliance was like a very costly stone, as a
> stone of crystal-clear jasper...And the city was
> pure gold, like clear glass...And I saw no temple
> in it, for the Lord God, the Almighty, and the
> Lamb, are its temple. And the city has no need
> of the sun or of the moon to shine upon it, for the
> glory of God has illumined it, and its lamp is the
> Lamb. And the nations shall walk by its light...
> and nothing unclean and no one who practices
> abomination and lying, shall ever come into it,
> but only those whose names are written in the
> Lamb's book of life. (Rev 21:2,9-11,18-27 NAS).

The last vision of the Church given in Scripture is of a
city in which every stone is perfectly fitted to every other,
and it is as clear as crystal, without the least shadow or haze.
Light flows through this Church unimpeded and undistorted.
It is completely visible to the world, not because it has lifted
itself up, not because it has mastered the arts of public rela-
tions and media exploitation, but because it is transparent,
true, and filled with light.

It has no need of natural light. The glory of God is its
illumination. And the lamp in which and through which that
light shines is the Lamb of God. It is Christ in His humility, in His meekness, as the Lamb of God, who sits upon the
throne and who fills the Church with living light. The light
of the Church by which the nations shall walk comes through
the humility of Christ. No unclean things, no abominations,
and no lies can come into it. No stone that deflects light onto
itself, that tries to possess and control and employ the light,
or to bend and shape it for its own ends can be a part of this
city. The Bride of the Lamb is without spot or wrinkle. She
is free from all guile. She is humble and true. She is the

glory of Christ, who is the glory of God. This is what God is preparing, stone by stone, and He will continue until He can look down upon us and rejoice to see His children walking in truth. Our destiny is to be more than merely "right." We are ordained to be filled with light. We need to set our sights on this goal, to glimpse the city descending out of heaven, and to seek the grace that is given to make us transparent stones, radiating the light and the glory and the truth of God. Amen.

OTHER BOOKS by Art Katz

REALITY: THE HOPE OF GLORY
The four messages in this book are a powerful inspiration to those who will not settle for less than the true meaning of life as a disciple of Christ.
Paperback, 156 pages.

BEN ISRAEL – ODYSSEY OF A MODERN JEW
Written as a literal journal, Art recounts his experience as an atheist and former Marxist being apprehended by a God whom he was not seeking. The message of this book has been powerfully used to bring other of Art's Jewish kinsmen to the faith of their fathers.
Paperback, 149 pages.

THE TEMPTATIONS OF CHRIST
– A Call to Sonship and Maturity
The scriptures indicate that Jesus was led into the wilderness in the fullness of the Spirit, but came out of that testing place in the power of the Spirit. The author examines the necessary progression in our Christian lives without which we will never be able to convey the knowledge of the risen Christ.
Paperback, 56 pages.

WHAT A JEW DOES WITH JESUS
Despite the apparent contradiction, the author pleads with his Jewish kinsmen to take into their deepest consideration the truth that biblical Judaism is determined solely by what we do with Jesus of Nazareth. Paperback, 128 pages.

TRUE FELLOWSHIP
– Church as Community
When God called us to establish a Christian community, I knew that it was a call to the cross, to humiliation and suffering. We were going to be living closely and intensively with other believers on a daily basis in which our defects, our shortcomings and our failures would be revealed. Out of the agonies and the joys, we gave opportunity for a reality to come forth that can best be described as "true fellowship." Paperback, 146 pages.

THE PROPHETIC CALL
– *True and False Prophets*
If we cannot distinguish between the prophets that are true and those that are false, it is a statement that we are unable to distinguish between the God who is true and the god who is false. Art seeks to identify the essential elements of what makes a prophet true, and by that, he gives a corresponding glimpse into the truth of God as He in fact is.
Paperback, 110 pages.

THE HOLOCAUST: WHERE WAS GOD?
– *An inquiry into the biblical roots of tragedy.*
In a daring hypothesis, the author turns to the ancient Hebrew scriptures as the key of interpretation to one of the most catastrophic events of modern times: the Jewish Holocaust of World War II. In this examination of that ultimate tragedy, the issue of God as God is brought courageously to the forefront of our modern consideration as few books have attempted to do. Paperback, 91 pages.

DACHAU – A SILENT WITNESS
Art takes up the subject of the silence of God during one of the darkest moments of Jewish calamity, and insists that the seeming absence of God, when rightly understood, is a key to the true knowledge of His reality and presence.
Booklet, 35 pages.

THE ANATOMY OF DECEPTION
In a dark and seductive age, and one that is increasingly abounding in deception and lying signs, the ability to discern between the false and the true is of paramount importance.
Paperback, 60 pages.

APOSTOLIC FOUNDATIONS
In his penetrating manner, Art shows that a church with apostolic foundations is a body of people whose central impulse is a radical and total jealousy for the glory of God. It was so at the church's inception, and needs to be so at its conclusion.
Paperback, 235 pages.